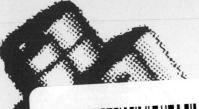

Story and art by
HIROYA OKU

DARK HORSE MANGA™

CONTENTS

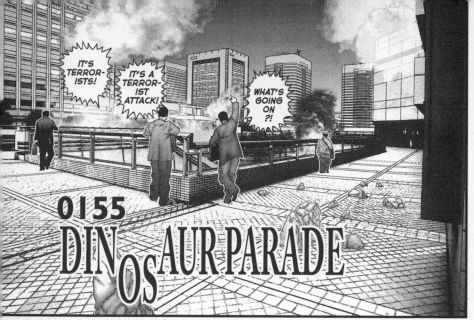

0155
DINOSAUR PARADE

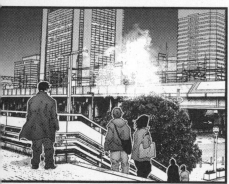

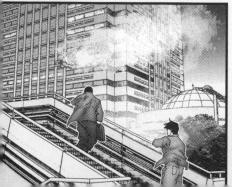

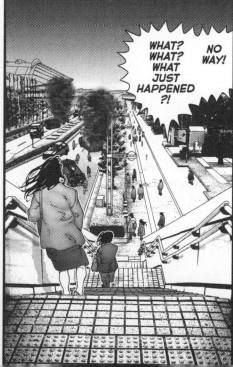

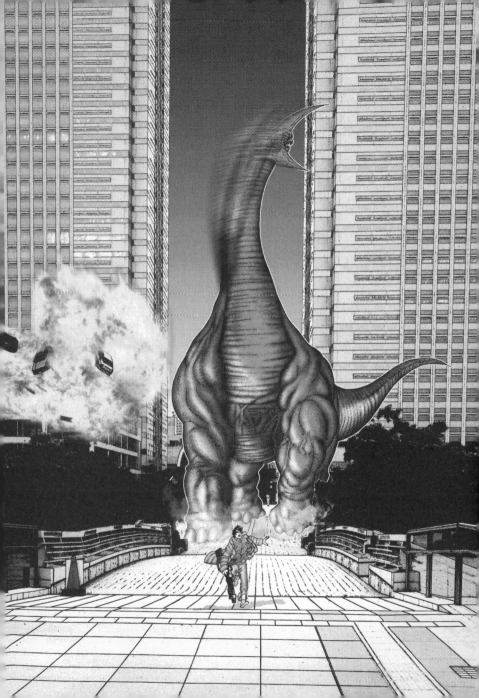

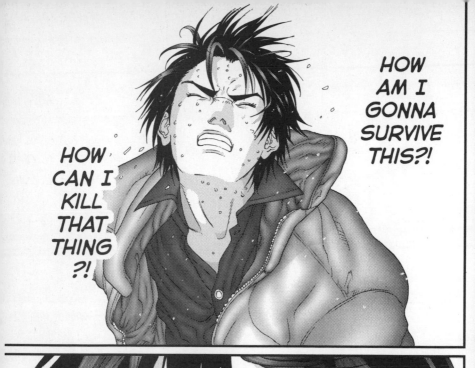

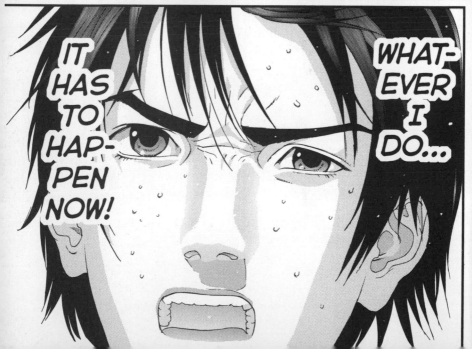

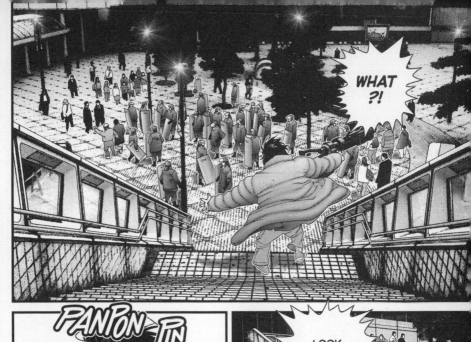

WHAT?!

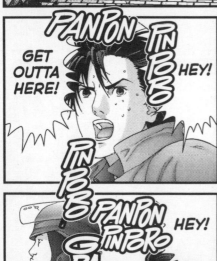

PANPON PINPORO

GET OUTTA HERE!

HEY!

PINPORO PANPON, PINPORO HEY!

GRAB

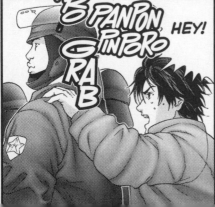

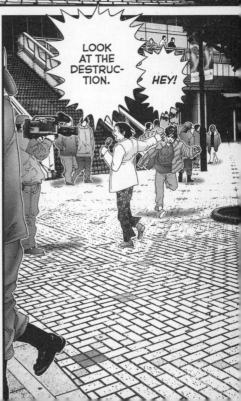

LOOK AT THE DESTRUC- TION.

HEY!

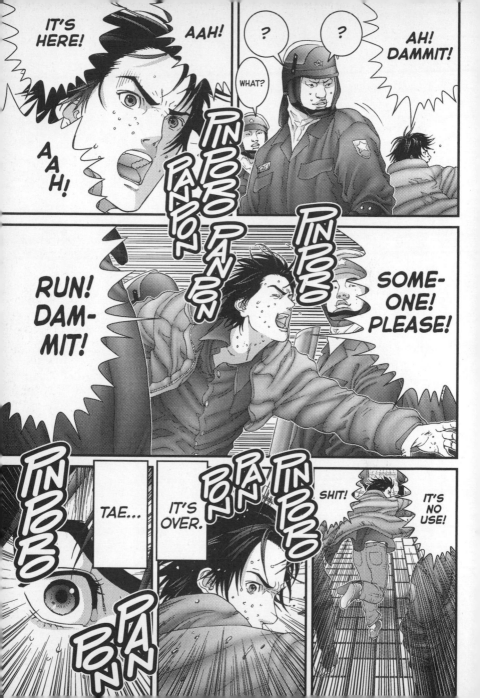

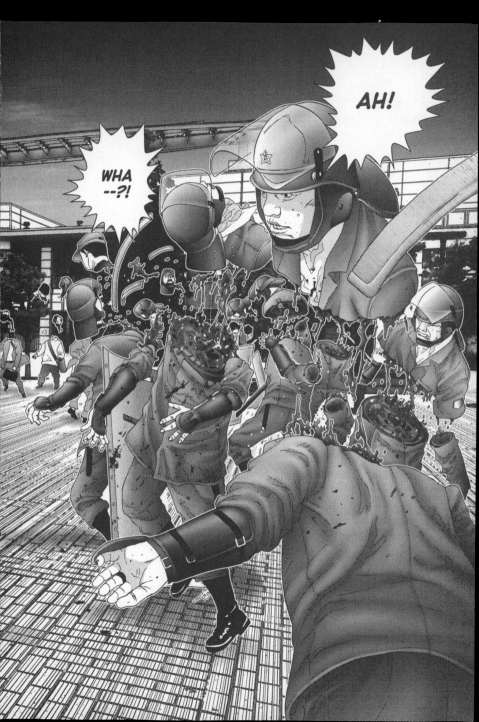

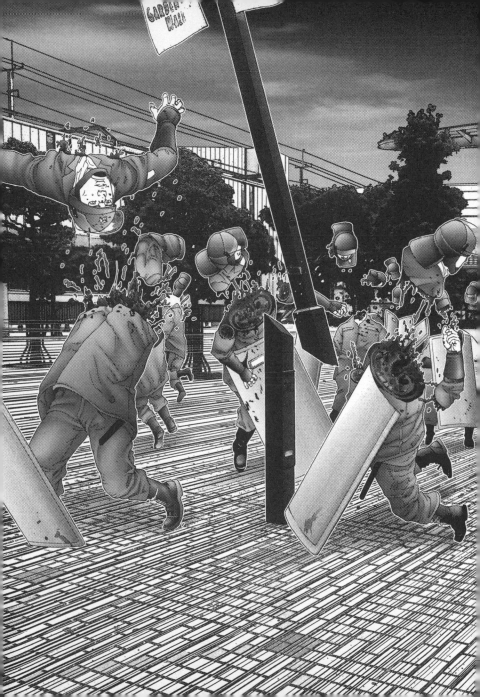

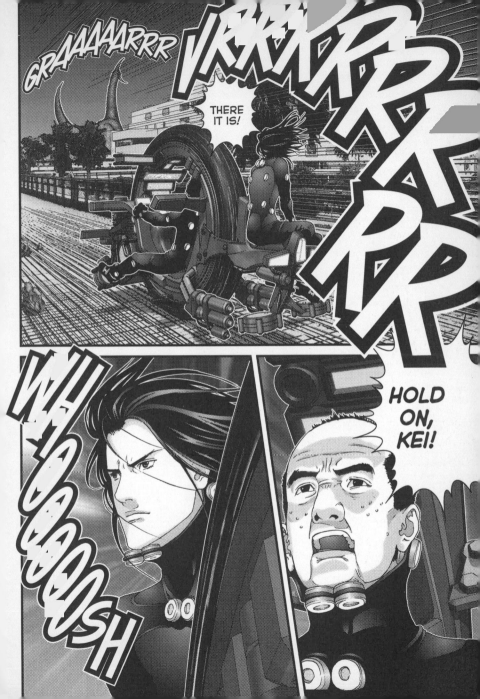

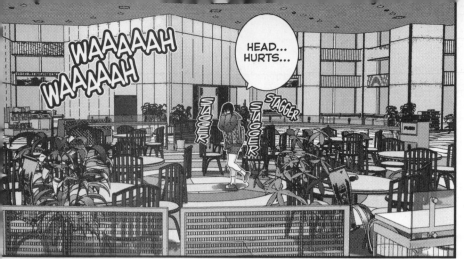

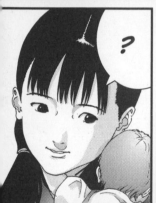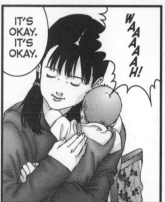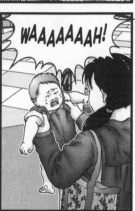

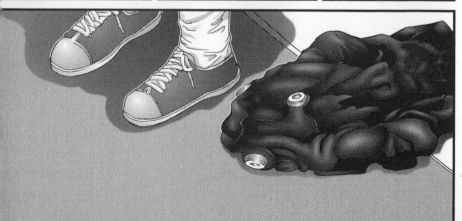

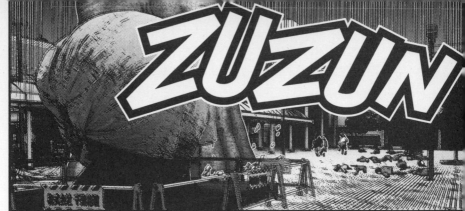

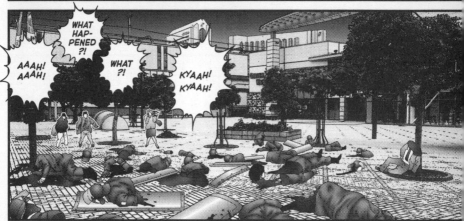

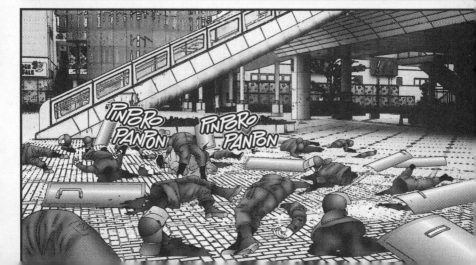

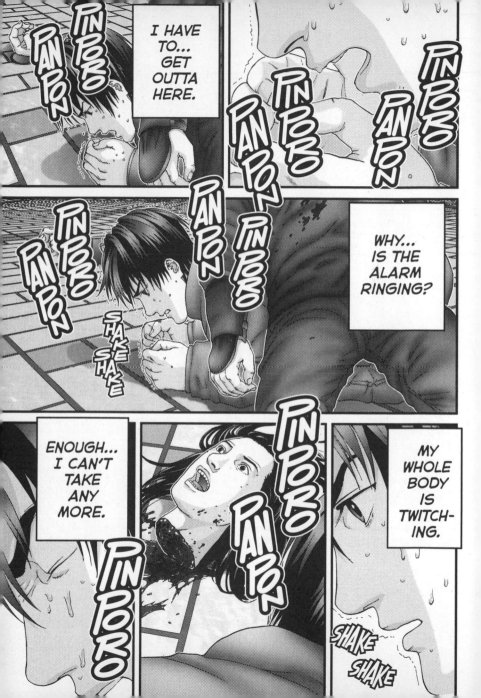

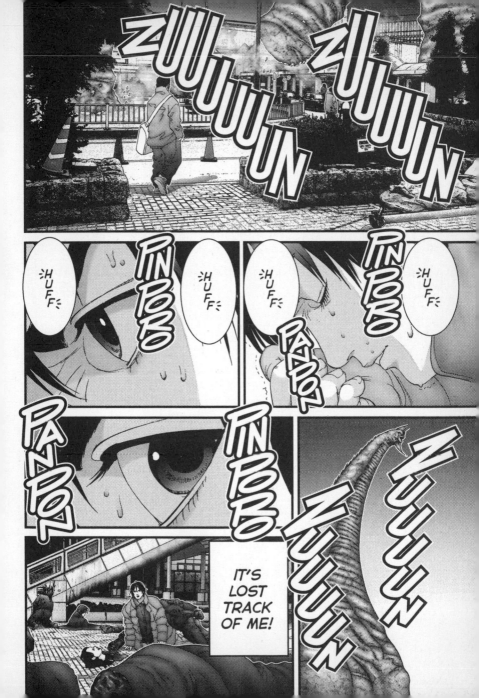

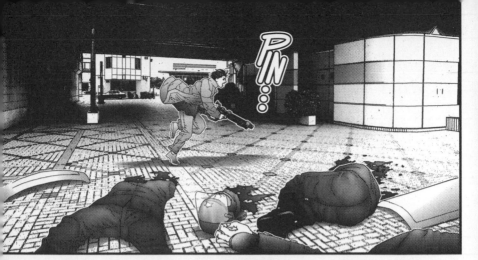

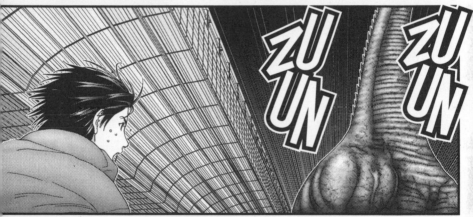

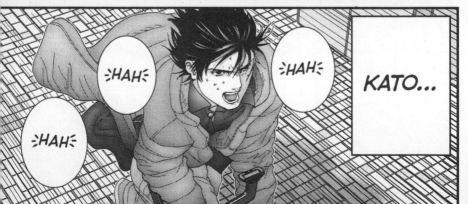

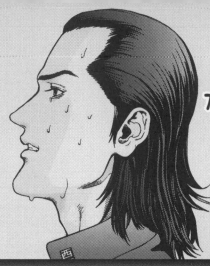

KATO. I ALWAYS THOUGHT HE WAS WEIRD.

I KINDA UNDERSTAND HIM NOW.

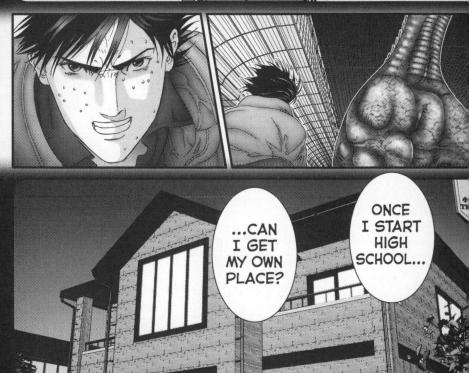

ONCE I START HIGH SCHOOL...

...CAN I GET MY OWN PLACE?

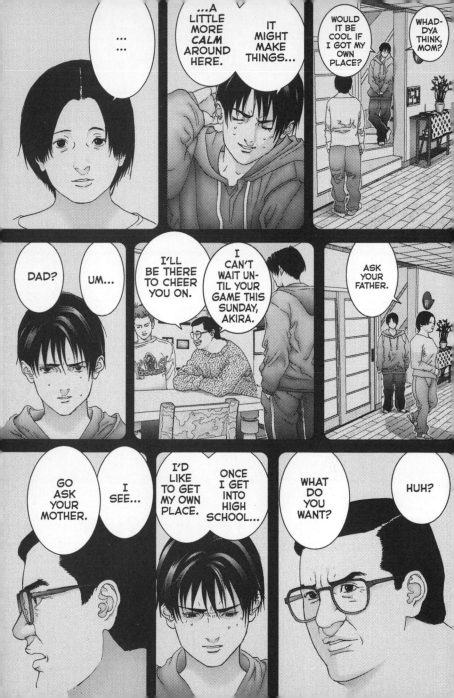

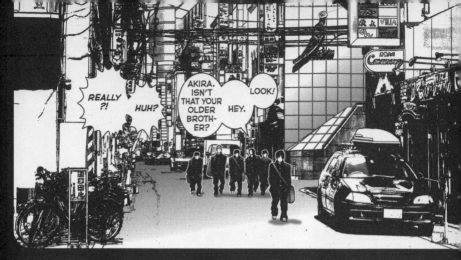

REALLY?! HUH? AKIRA. ISN'T THAT YOUR OLDER BROTHER? HEY. LOOK!

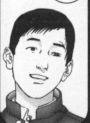

...KINDA DIFFICULT. HE'S... YOU KNOW... GUESS YOU DON'T GET ALONG.

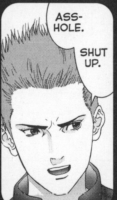

ASSHOLE. SHUT UP.

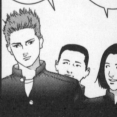

SHOULD WE ASK HIM TO JOIN US? HE'S SHORTER THAN YOU.

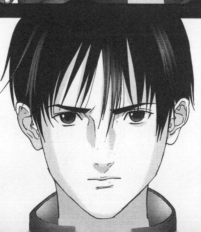

I HAVE NO IDEA WHAT'S GOIN' ON IN HIS HEAD.

HE'S ALWAYS SO DARK.

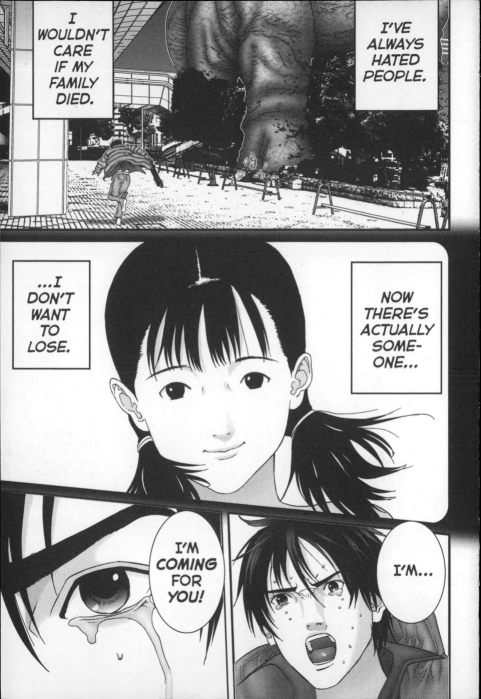

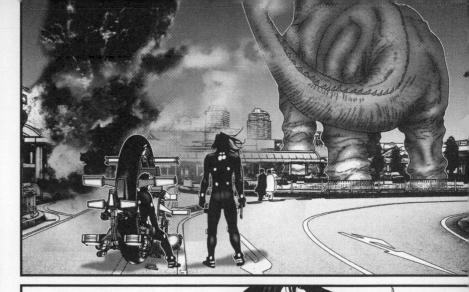

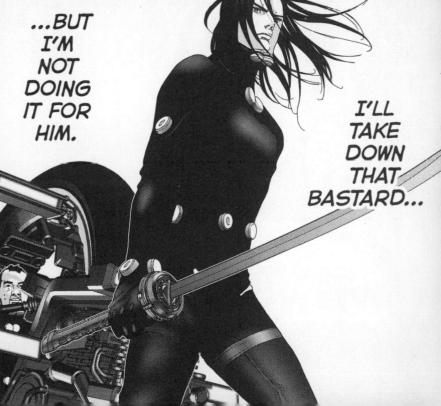

...BUT I'M NOT DOING IT FOR HIM.

I'LL TAKE DOWN THAT BASTARD...

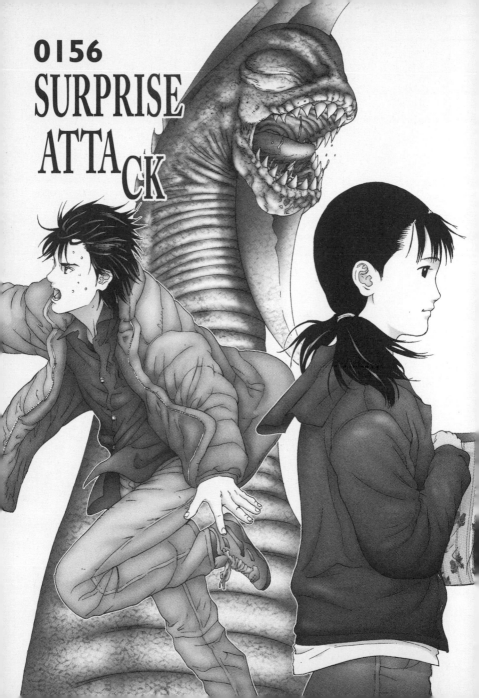

0156
SURPRISE
ATTACK

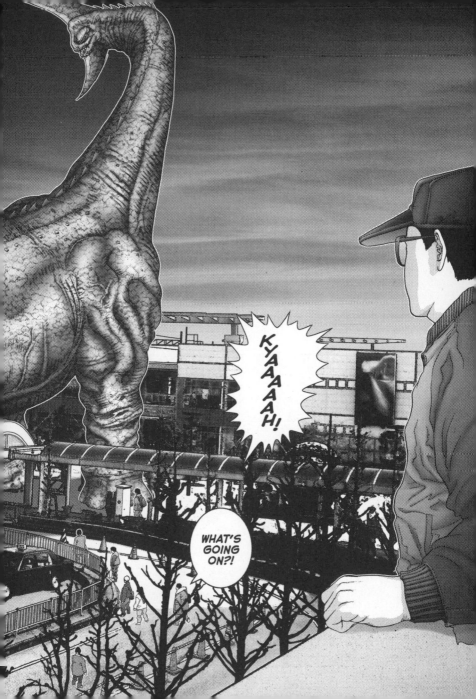

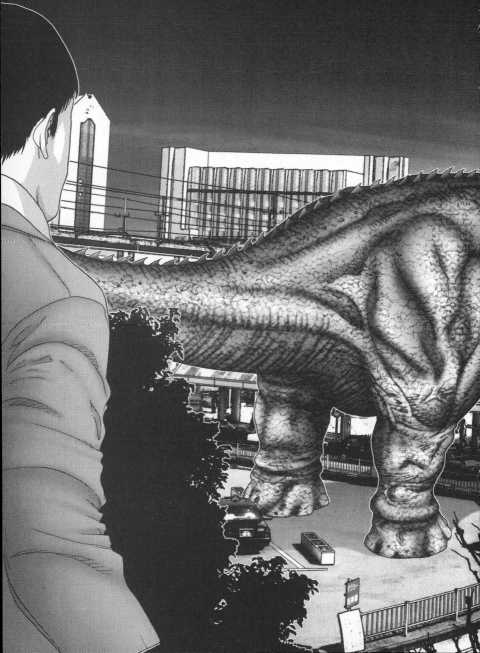

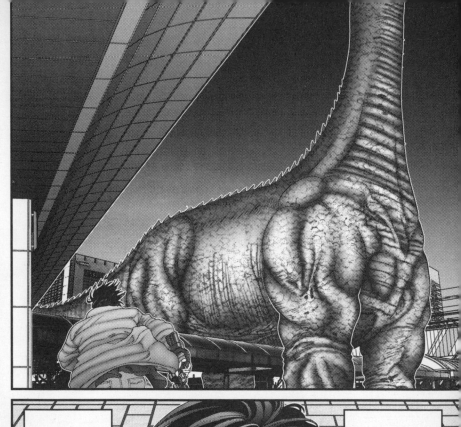

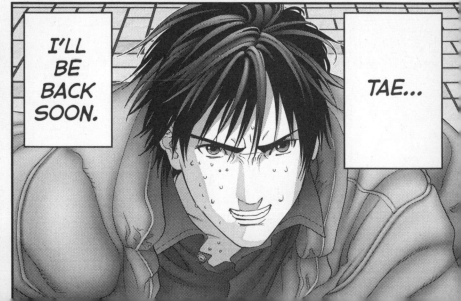

I'LL BE BACK SOON.

TAE...

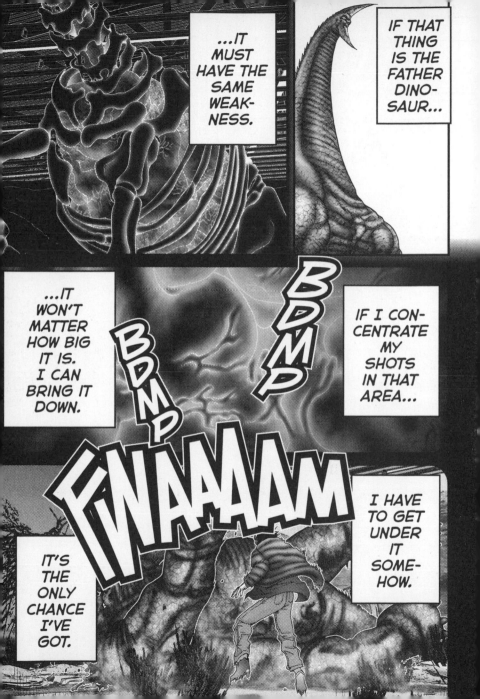

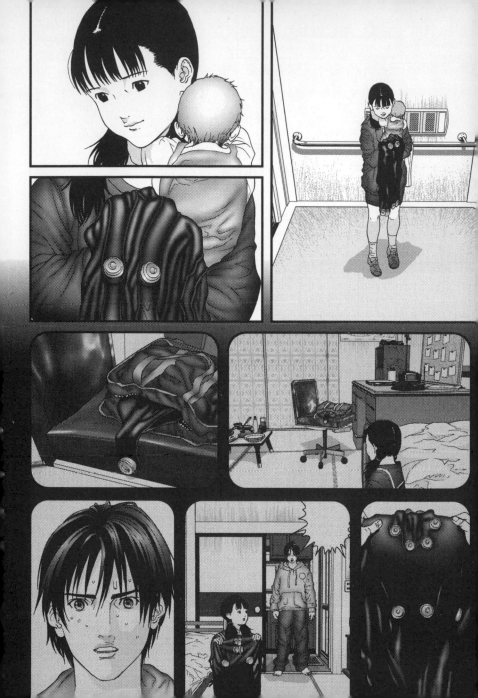

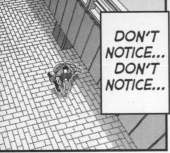

DON'T
NOTICE...
DON'T
NOTICE...

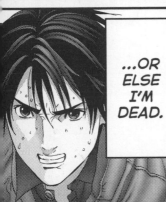

...OR
ELSE
I'M
DEAD.

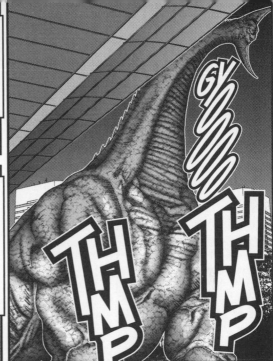

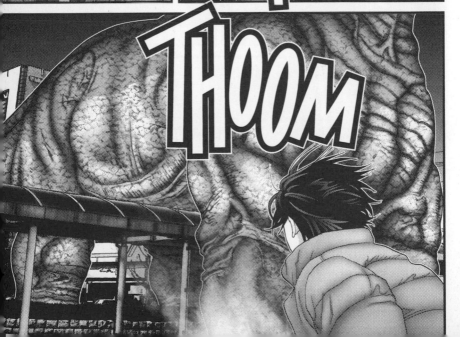

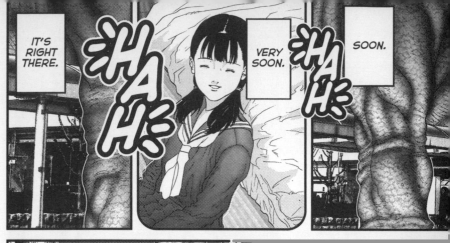

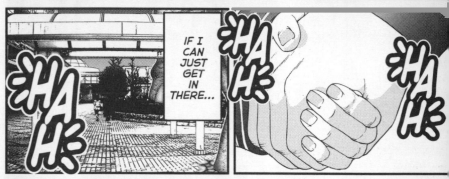

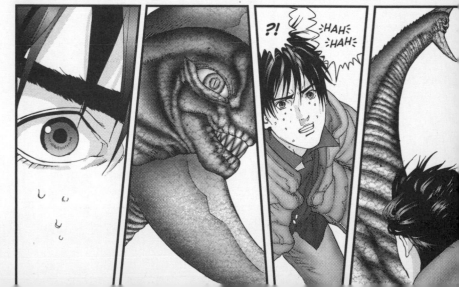

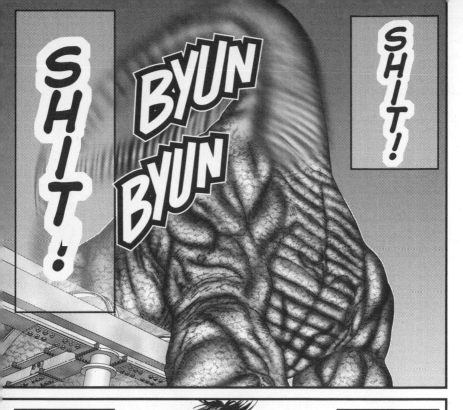
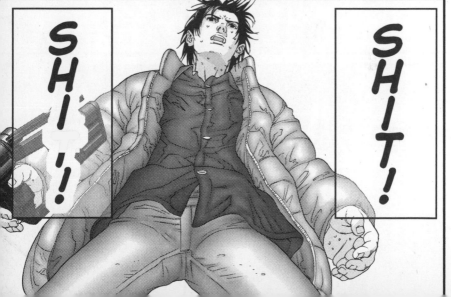

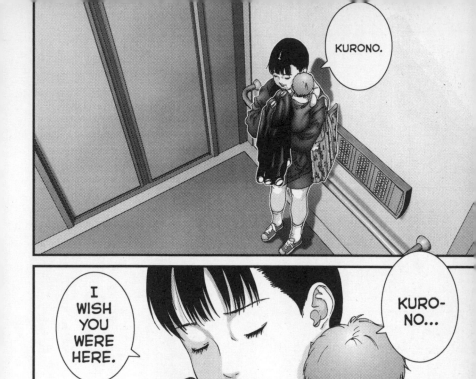
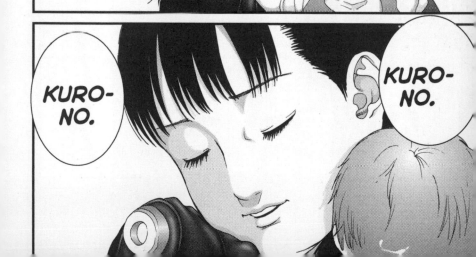

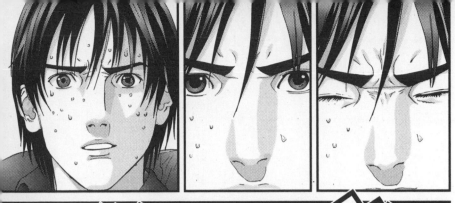

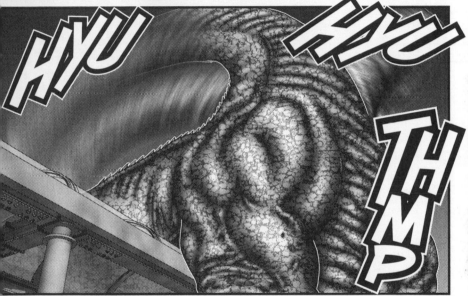

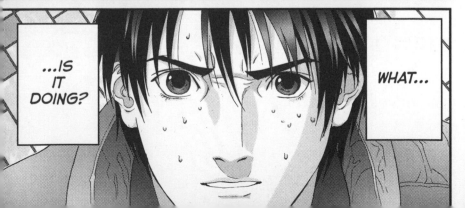

...IS IT DOING?

WHAT...

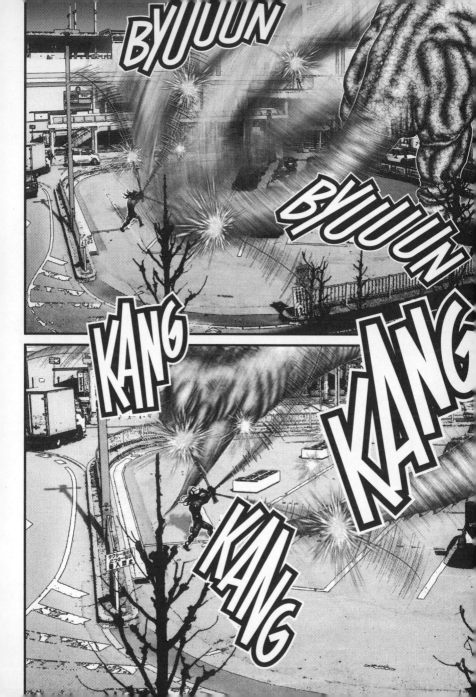

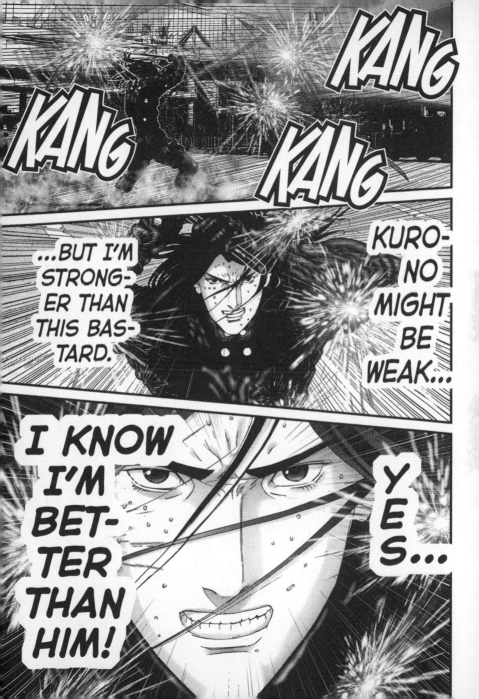

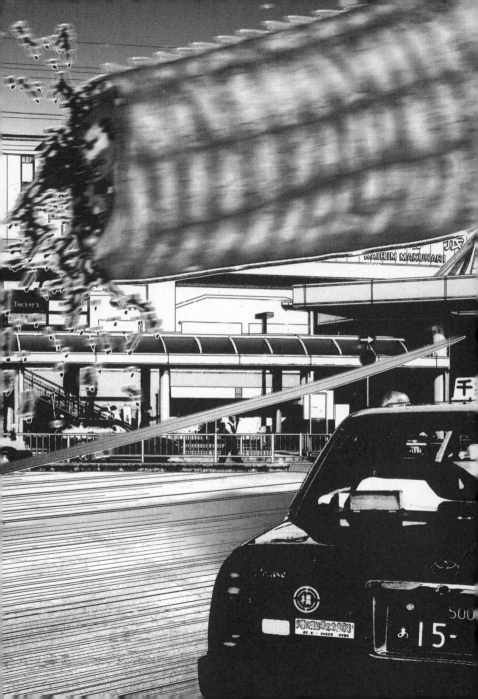

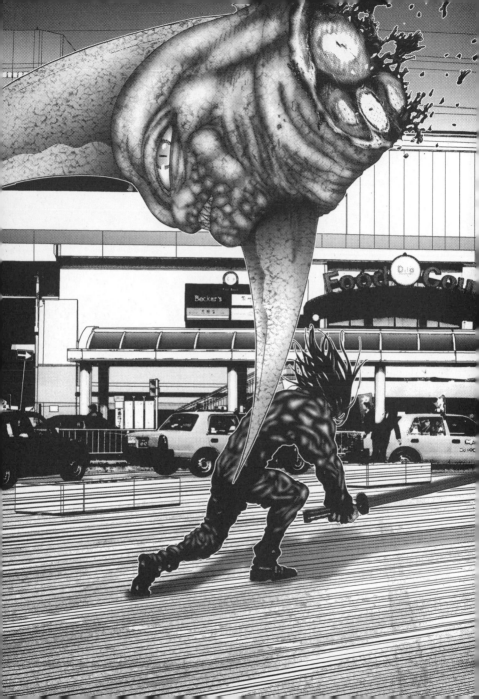

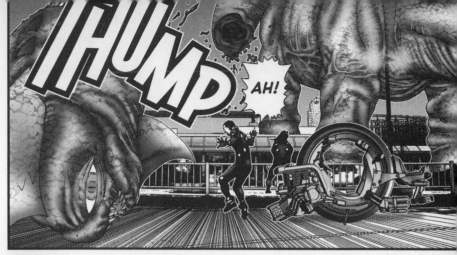

THUMP

AH!

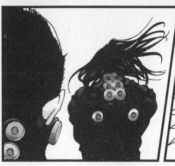

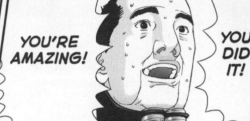

YOU'RE AMAZING!

YOU DID IT!

NOT YET!

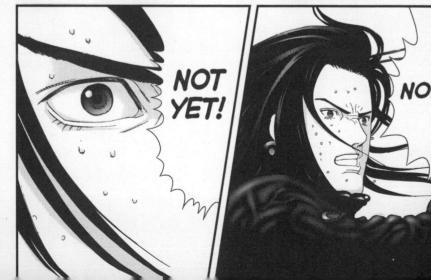

NO!

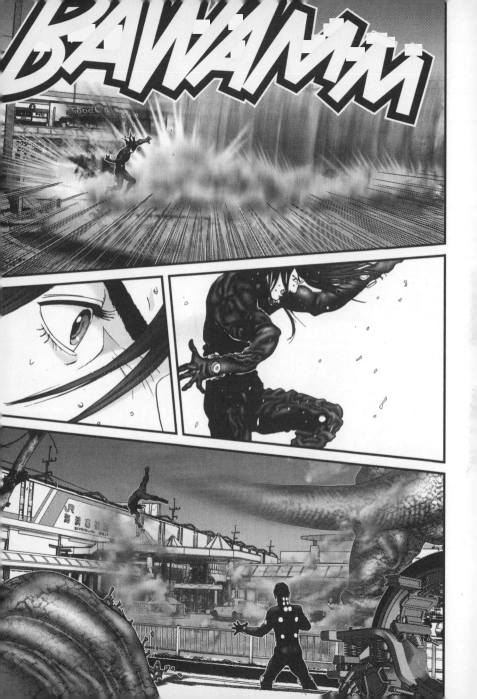

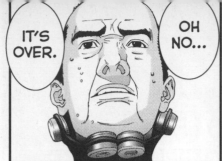

IT'S OVER.

OH NO...

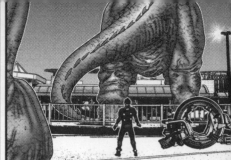

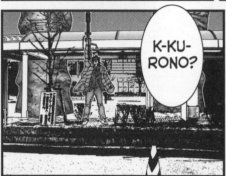

K-KU-RONO?

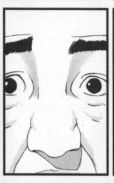

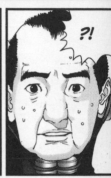

?!

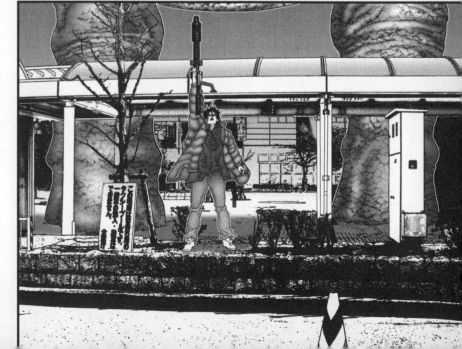

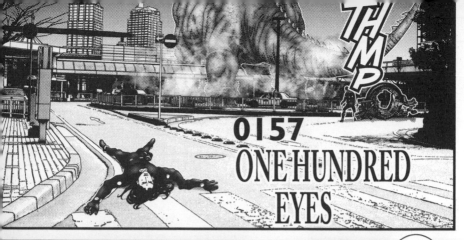

0157
ONE HUNDRED
EYES

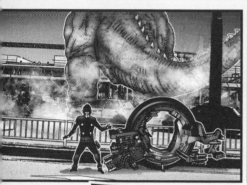

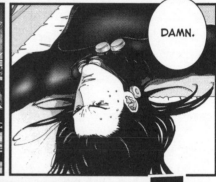

DAMN.

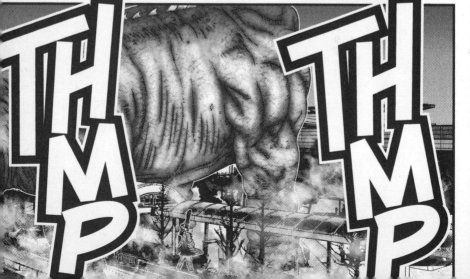

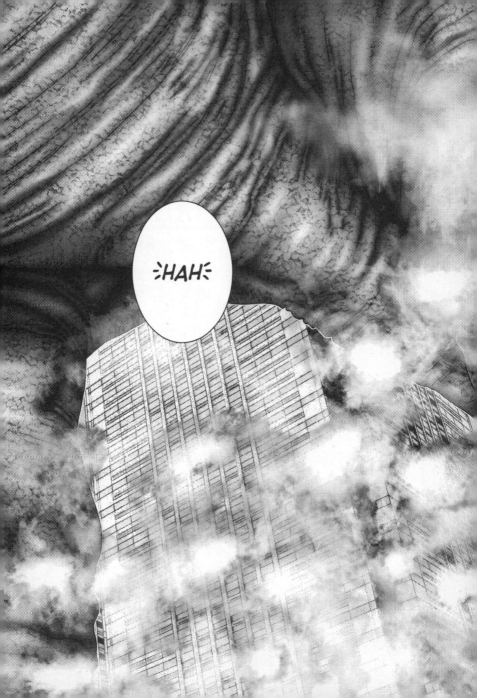

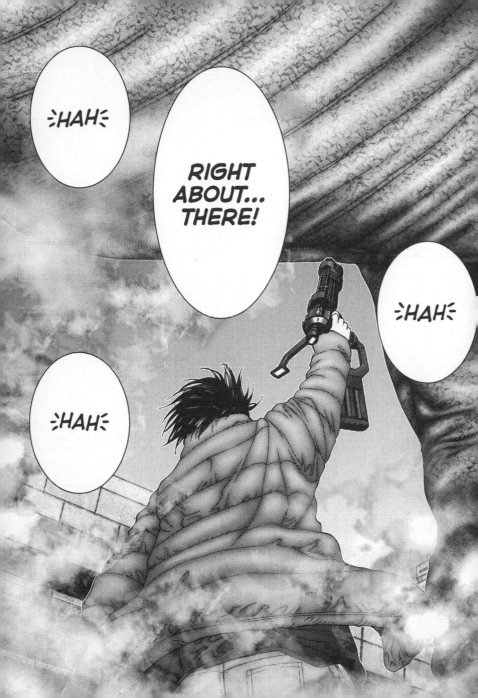

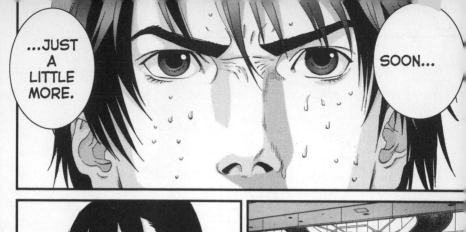

...JUST A LITTLE MORE.

SOON...

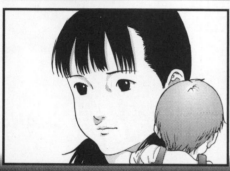

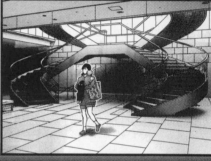

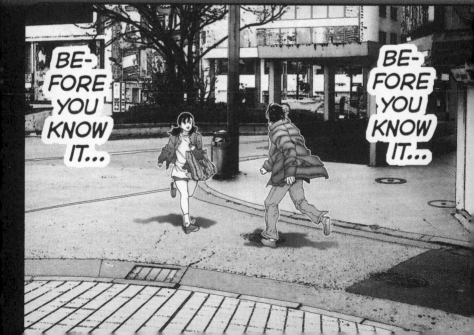

BE-FORE YOU KNOW IT...

BE-FORE YOU KNOW IT...

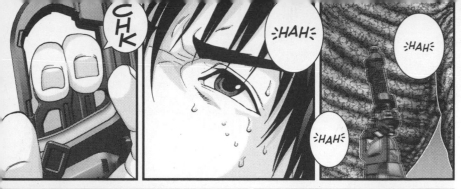

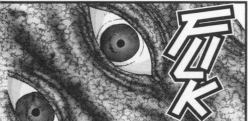

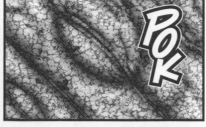

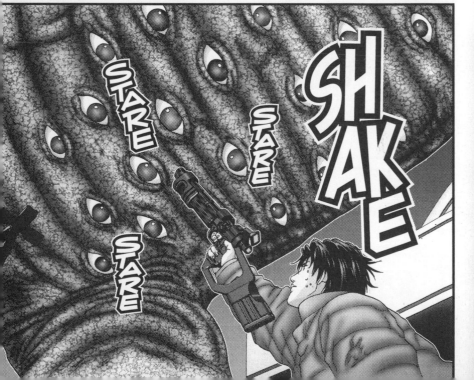

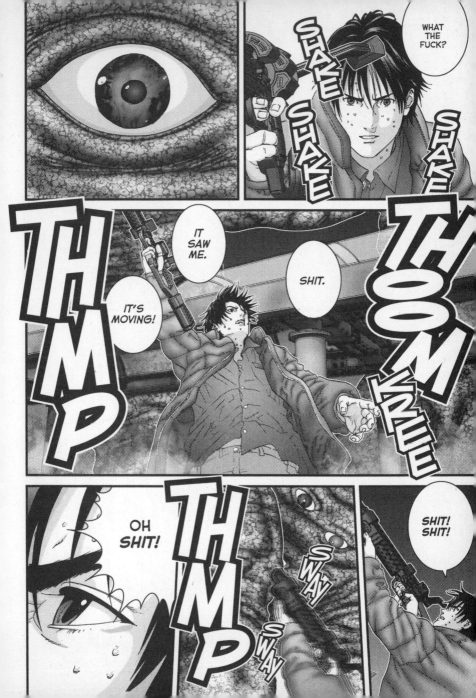

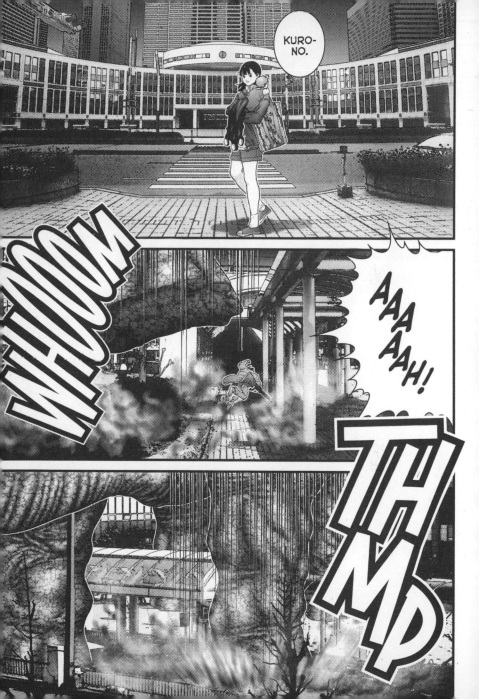

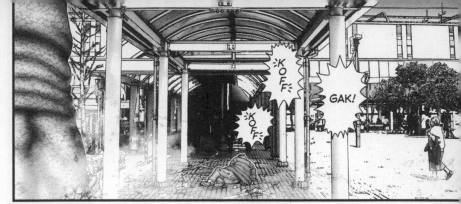

KOFF

KOFF

GAK!

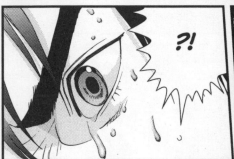

?!

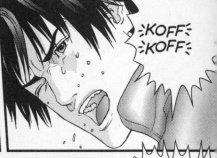

KOFF
KOFF

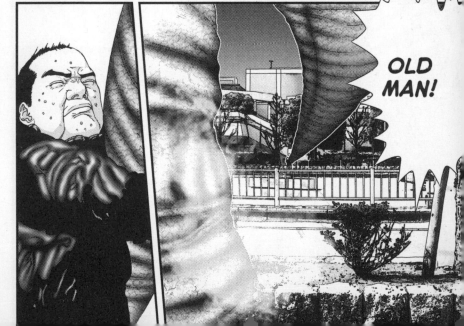

OLD MAN!

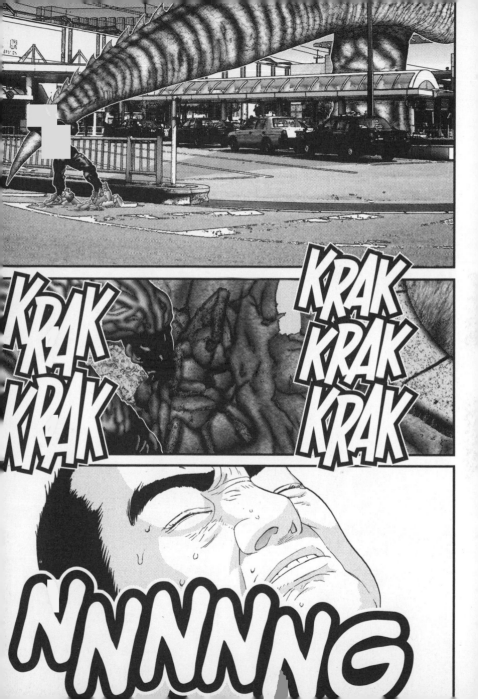

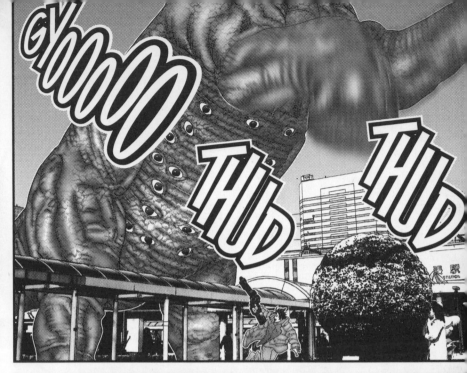

GYOOOOO

THUD

THUD

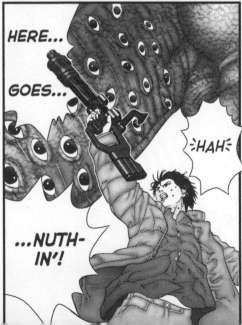

HERE...

GOES...

≡HAH≡

...NUTH-IN'!

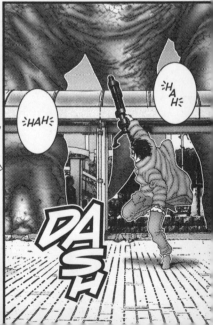

≡HAH≡

≡HAH≡

DASH

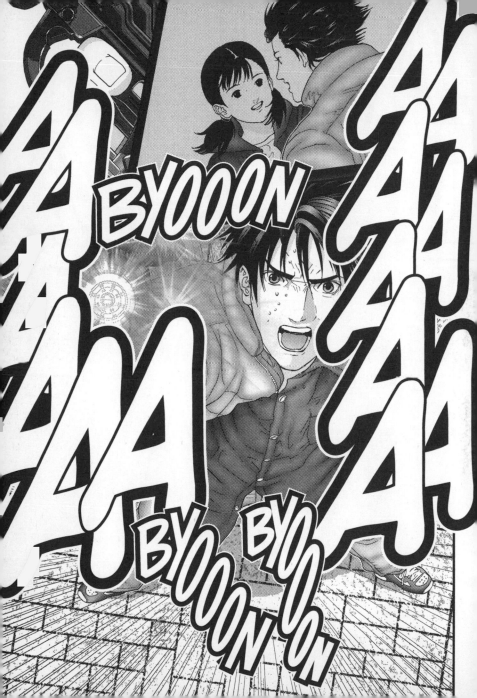

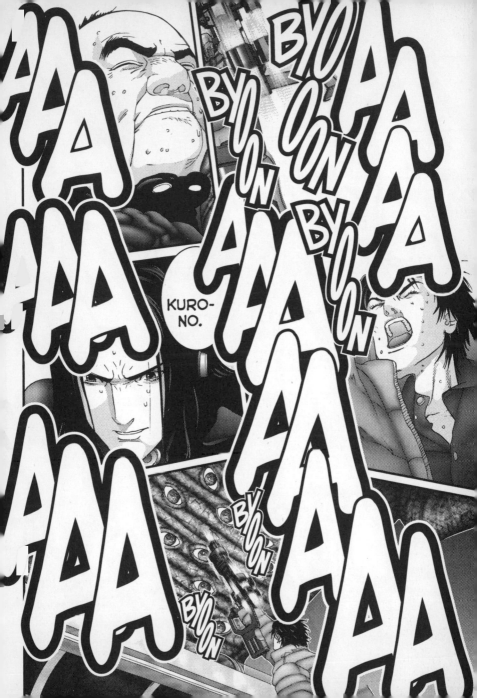

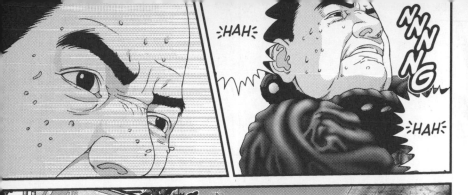

=HAH=

NNNNG

=HAH=

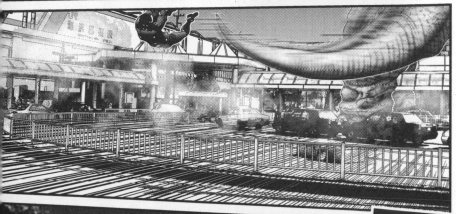

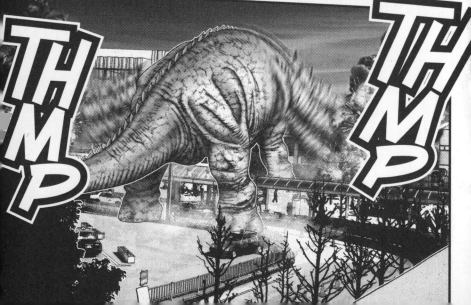

THMP

THMP

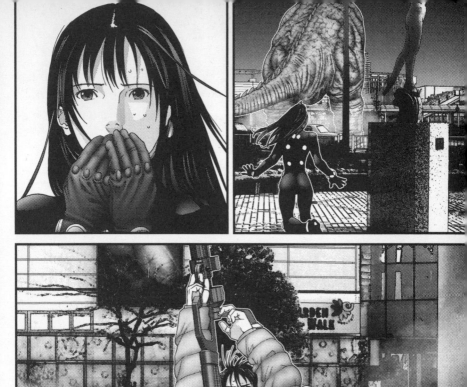

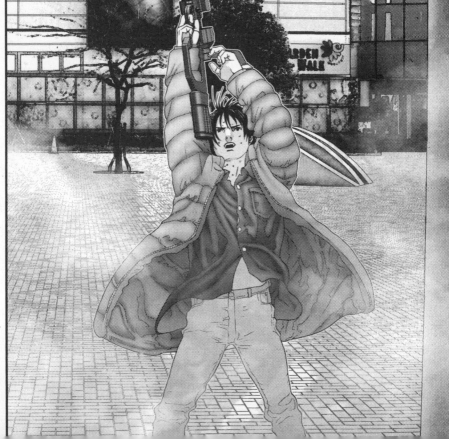

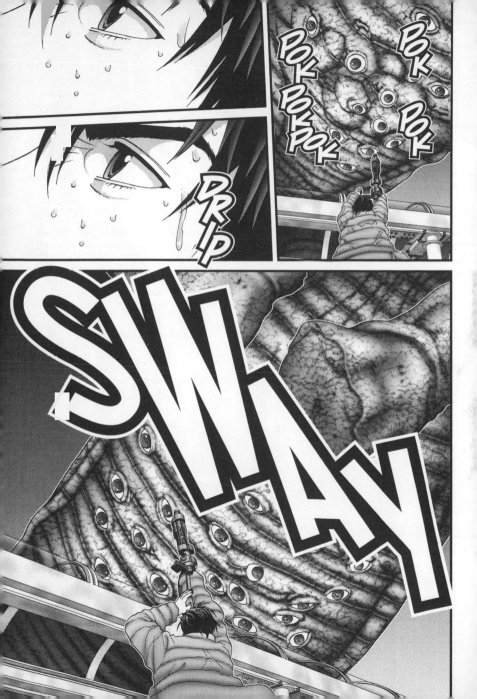

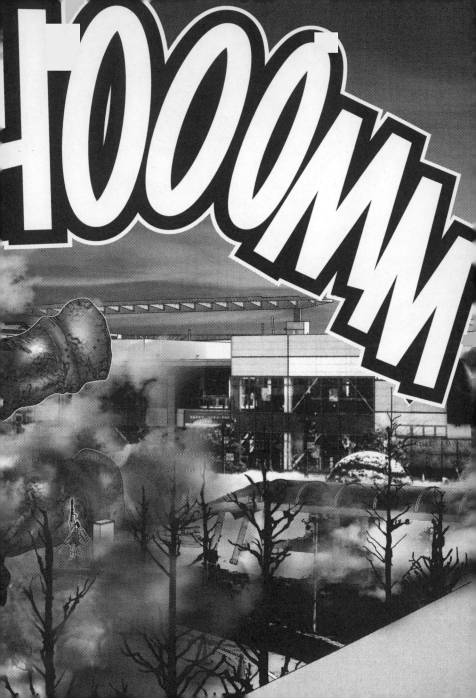

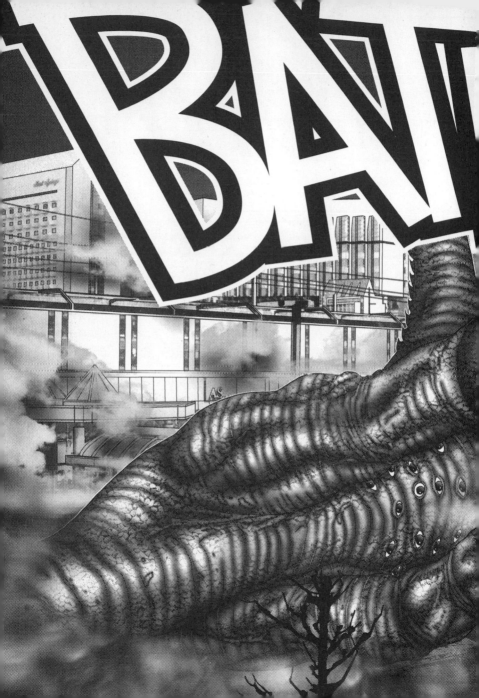

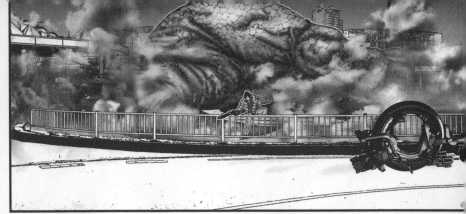

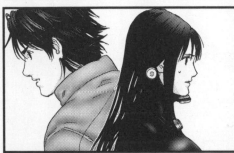

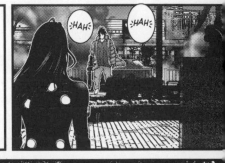

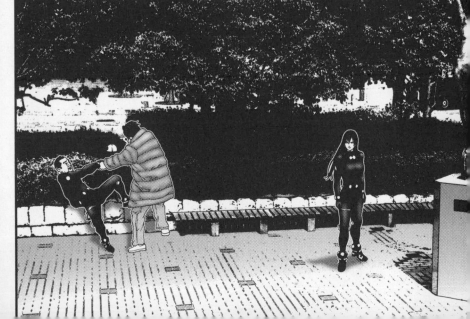

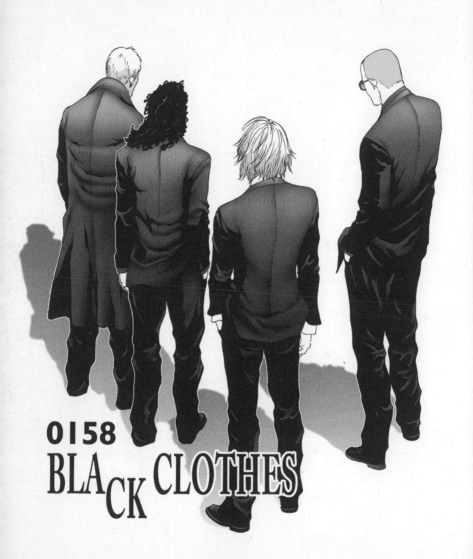

0158
BLACK CLOTHES

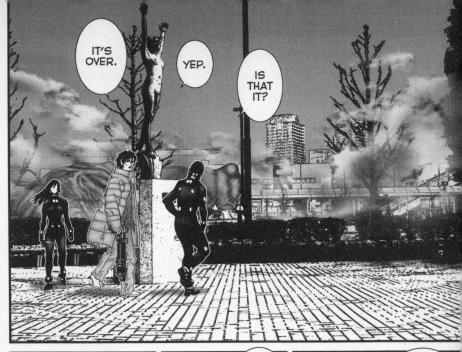

IT'S OVER.

YEP.

IS THAT IT?

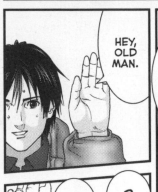

HEY, OLD MAN.

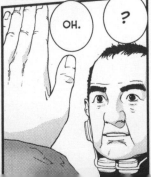

OH.

?

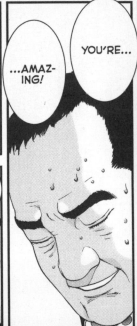

...AMAZ-ING!

YOU'RE...

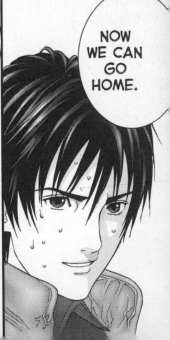

NOW WE CAN GO HOME.

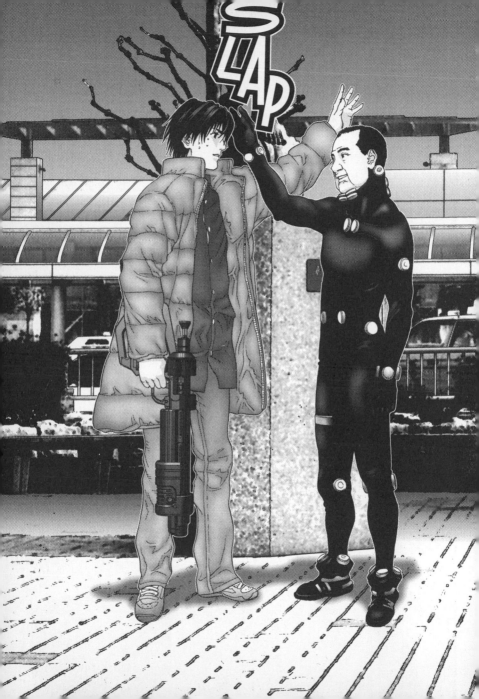

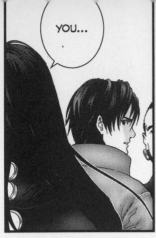

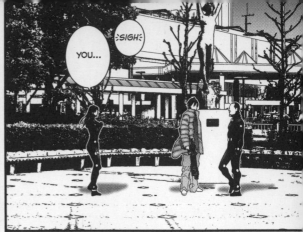

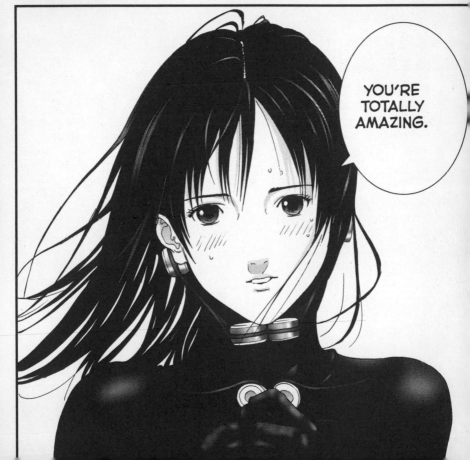

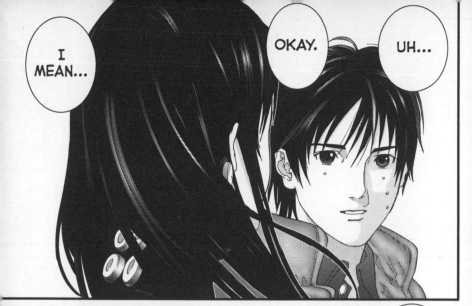

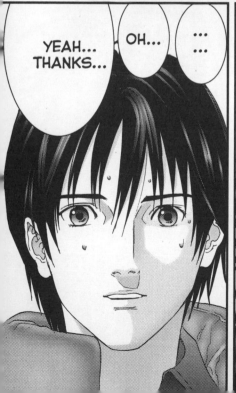

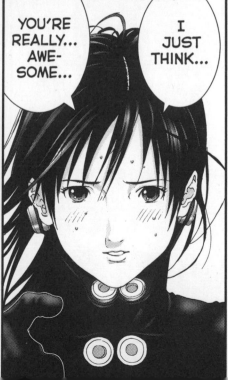

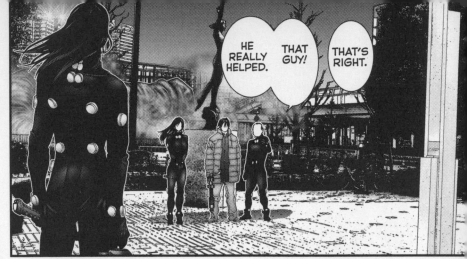

HE REALLY HELPED.

THAT GUY!

THAT'S RIGHT.

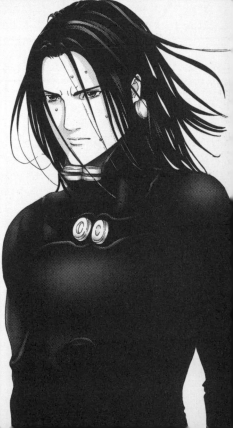

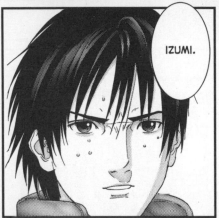

IZUMI.

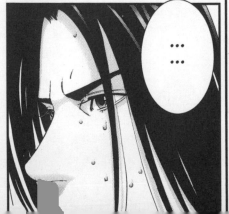

...
...

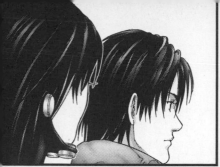

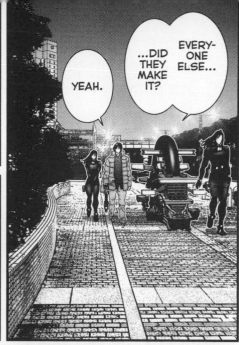

EVERY-ONE ELSE...

...DID THEY MAKE IT?

YEAH.

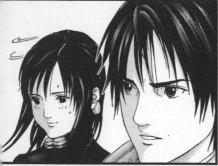

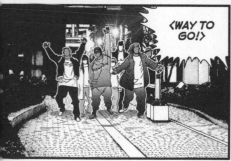

⟨WAY TO GO!⟩

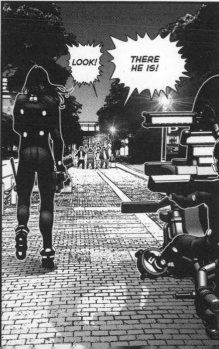

LOOK!

THERE HE IS!

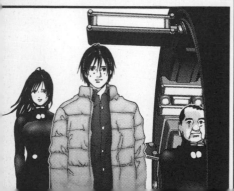

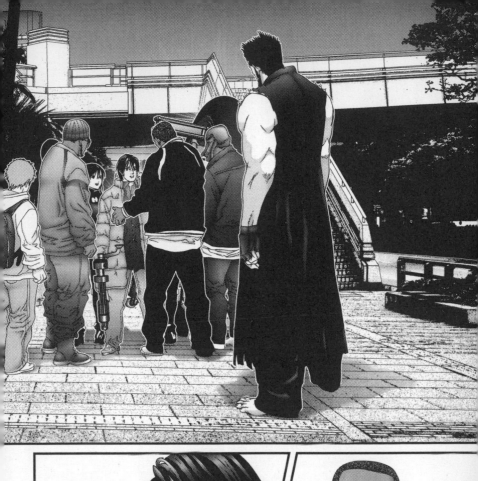
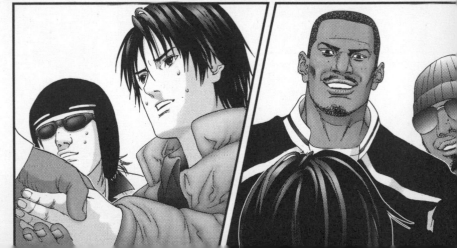

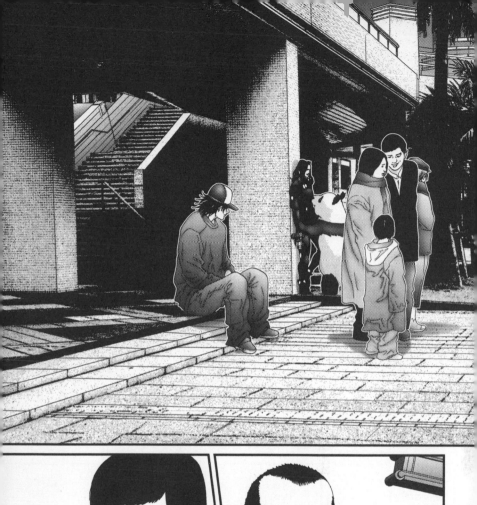
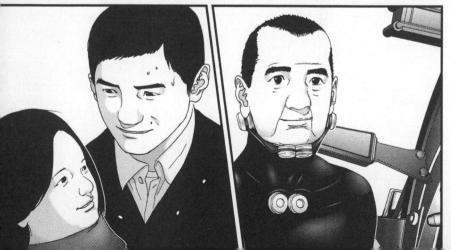

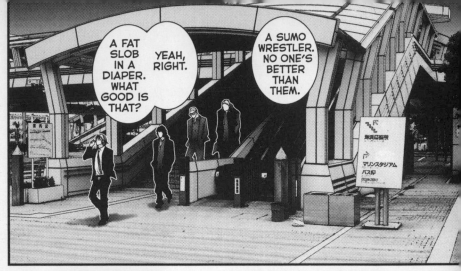

A FAT SLOB IN A DIAPER. WHAT GOOD IS THAT?

YEAH, RIGHT.

A SUMO WRESTLER. NO ONE'S BETTER THAN THEM.

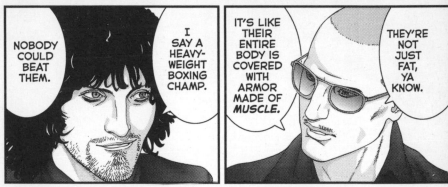

NOBODY COULD BEAT THEM.

I SAY A HEAVY-WEIGHT BOXING CHAMP.

IT'S LIKE THEIR ENTIRE BODY IS COVERED WITH ARMOR MADE OF *MUSCLE.*

THEY'RE NOT JUST FAT, YA KNOW.

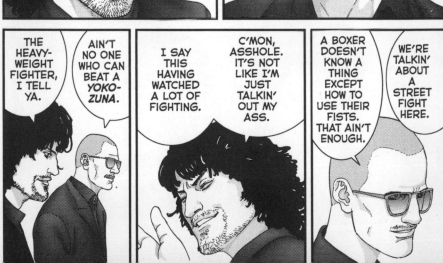

THE HEAVY-WEIGHT FIGHTER, I TELL YA.

AIN'T NO ONE WHO CAN BEAT A *YOKO-ZUNA.*

I SAY THIS HAVING WATCHED A LOT OF FIGHTING.

C'MON, ASSHOLE. IT'S NOT LIKE I'M JUST TALKIN' OUT MY ASS.

A BOXER DOESN'T KNOW A THING EXCEPT HOW TO USE THEIR FISTS. THAT AIN'T ENOUGH.

WE'RE TALKIN' ABOUT A STREET FIGHT HERE.

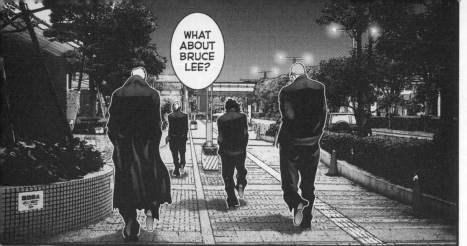

WHAT ABOUT BRUCE LEE?

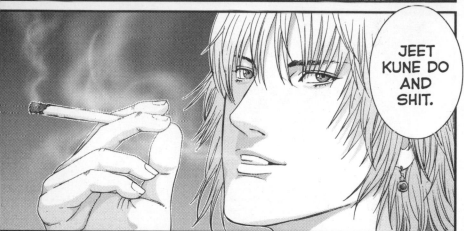

JEET KUNE DO AND SHIT.

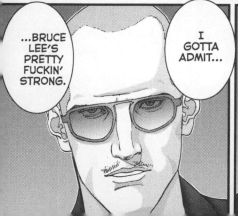

...BRUCE LEE'S PRETTY FUCKIN' STRONG.

I GOTTA ADMIT...

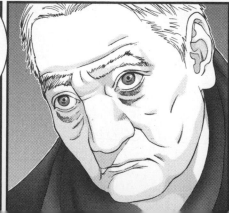

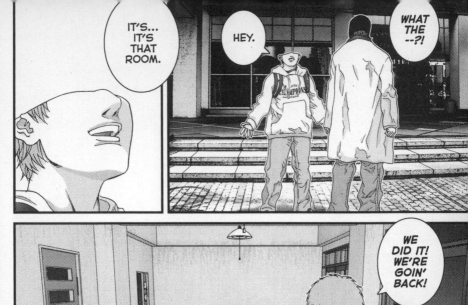

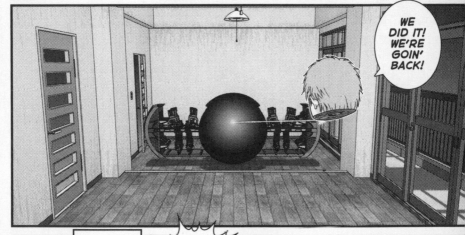

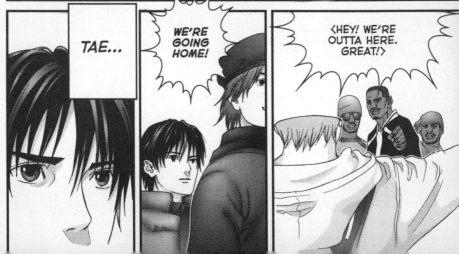

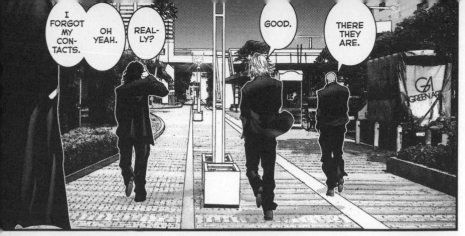

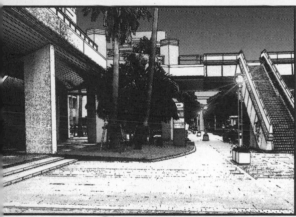

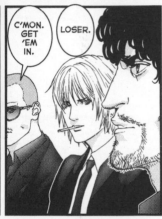

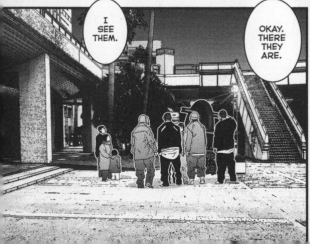

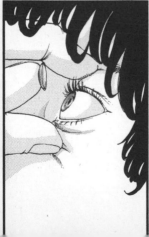

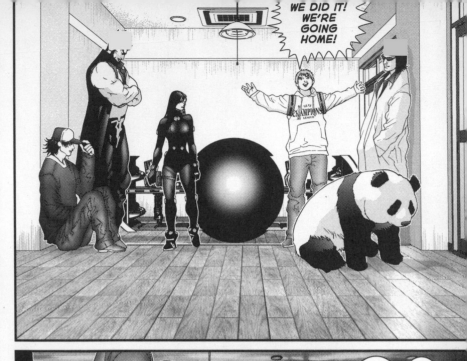

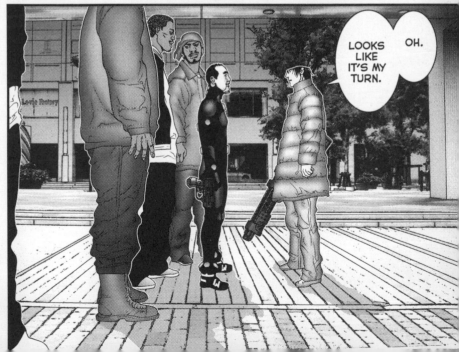

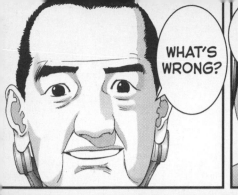

WHAT'S WRONG?

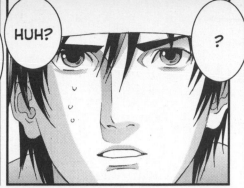

HUH?

?

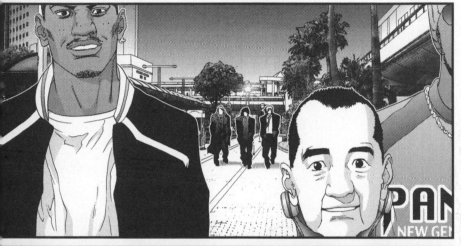

PAN
NEW GE

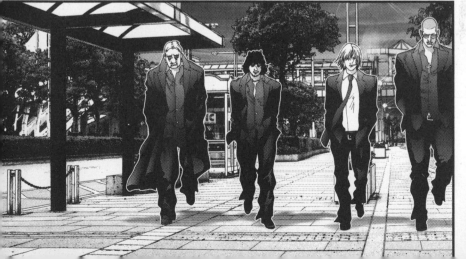

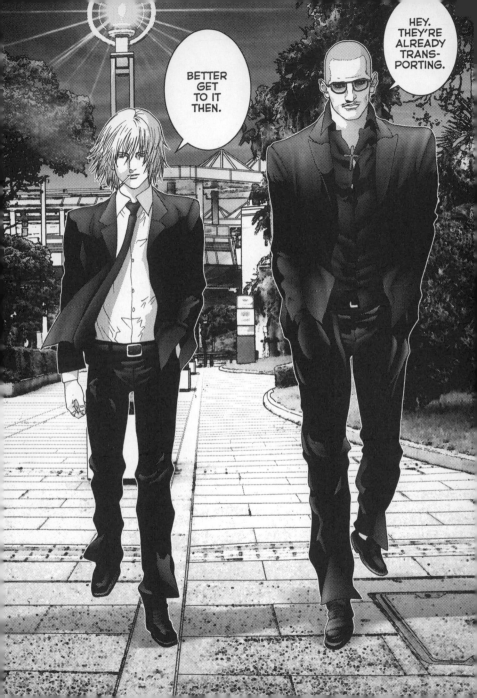

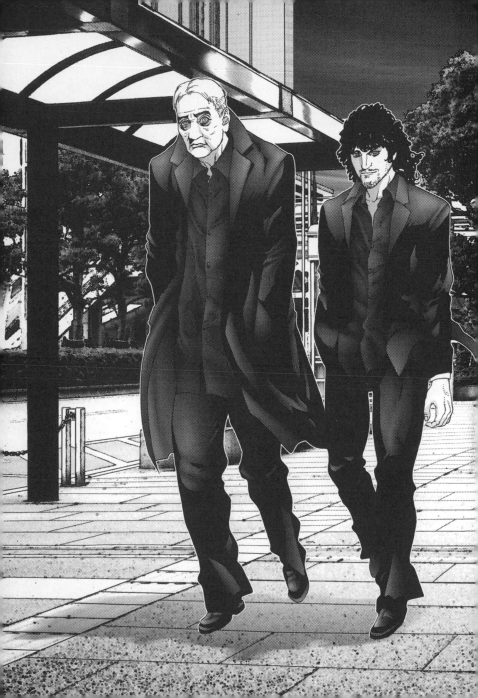

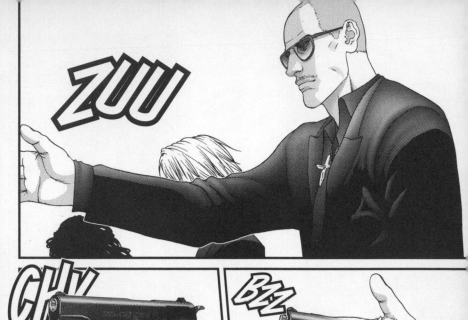

ZUU

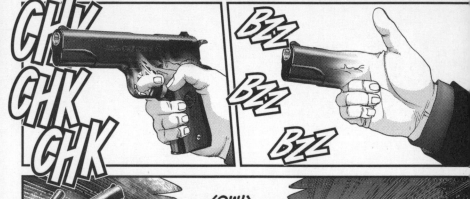

CHK CHK CHK

BZZ BZZ BZZ

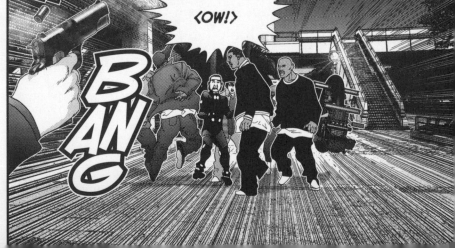

‹OW!›

BANG

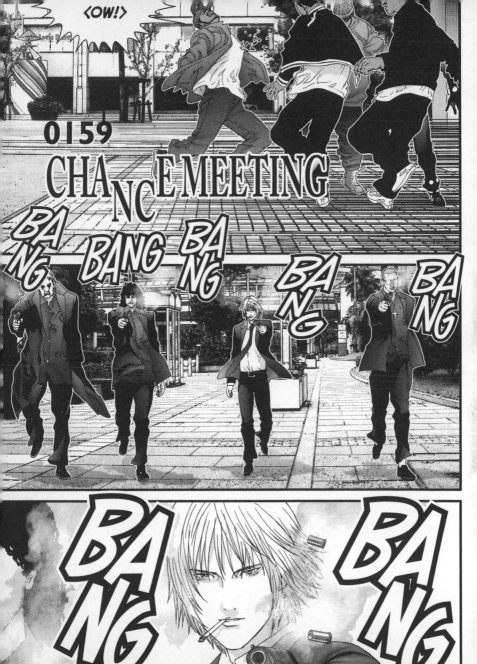

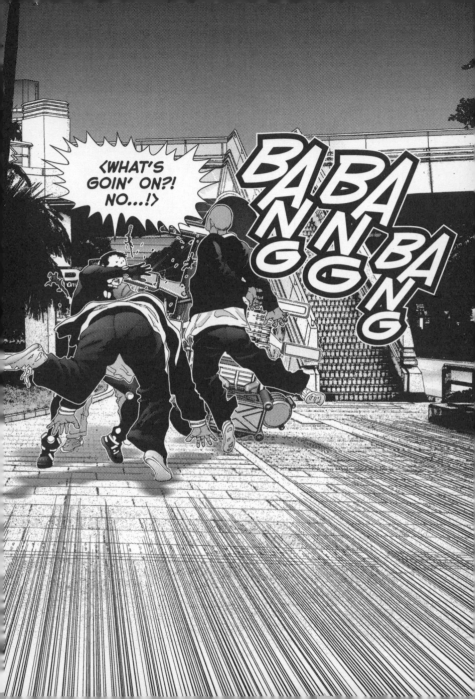

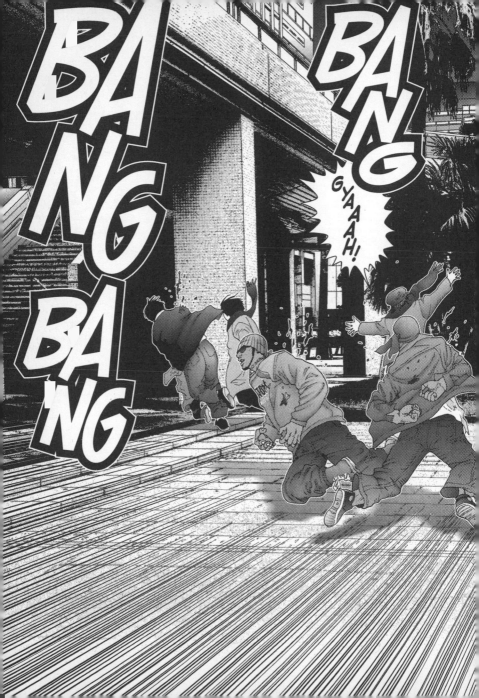

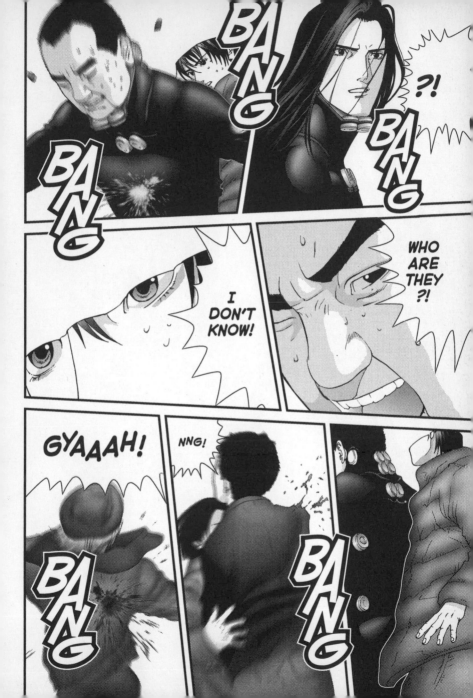

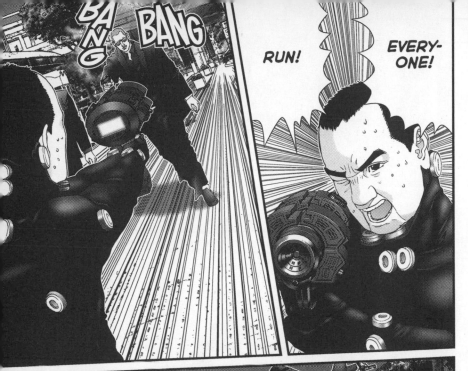

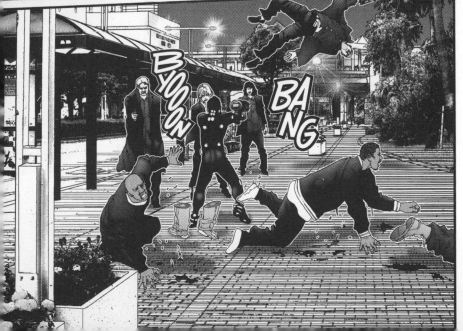

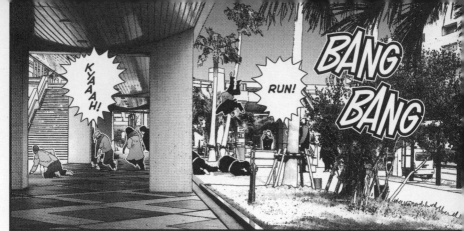

KYAAAH!

RUN!

BANG BANG

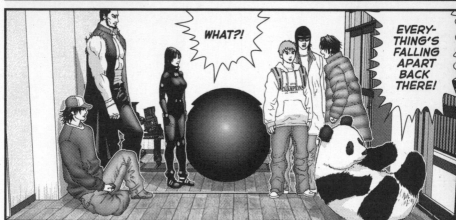

WHAT?!

EVERY-THING'S FALLING APART BACK THERE!

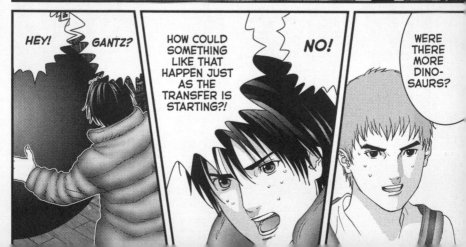

HEY! GANTZ?

HOW COULD SOMETHING LIKE THAT HAPPEN JUST AS THE TRANSFER IS STARTING?!

NO!

WERE THERE MORE DINO-SAURS?

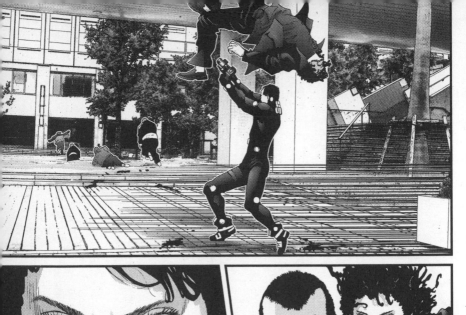

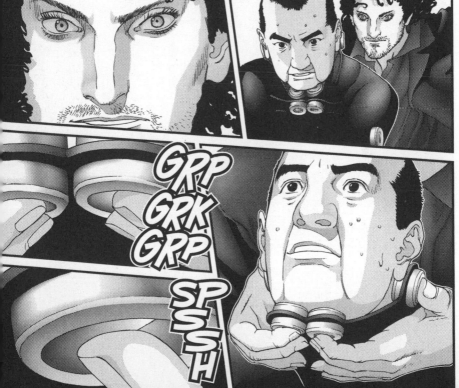

GRP
GRK
GRP

SPSSH

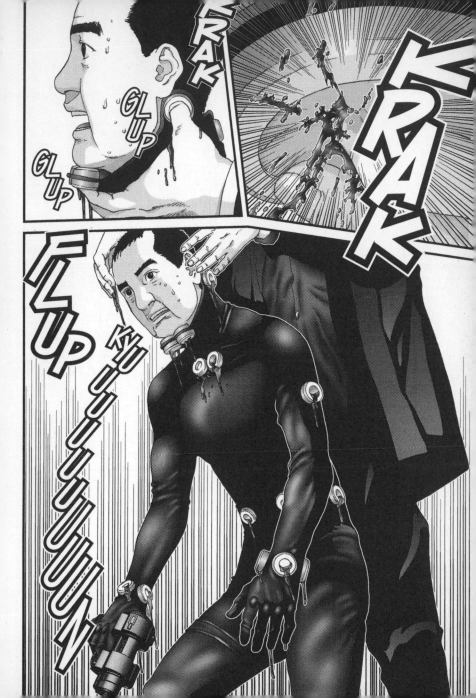

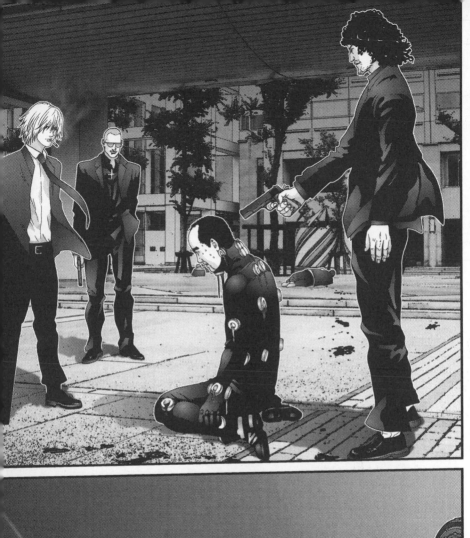

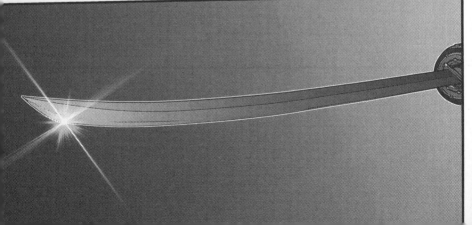

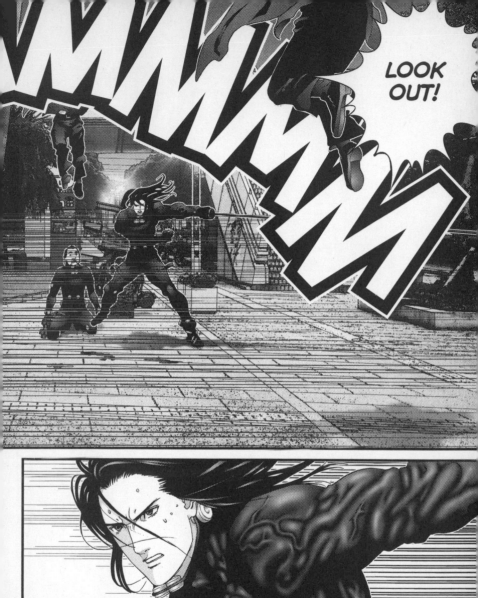

LOOK OUT!

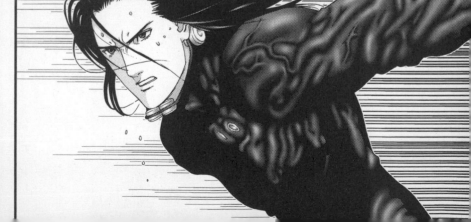

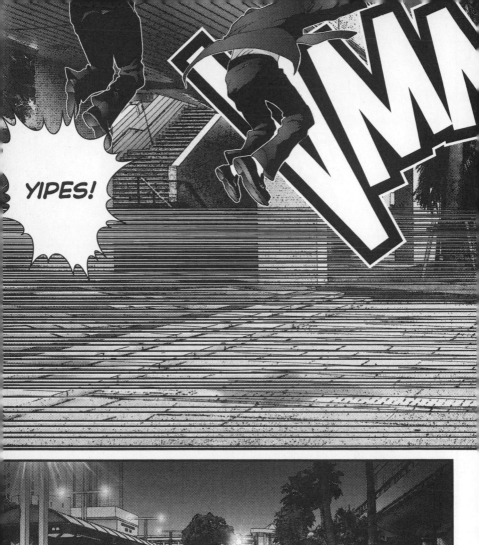

YIPES!

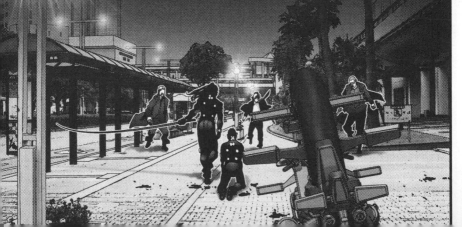

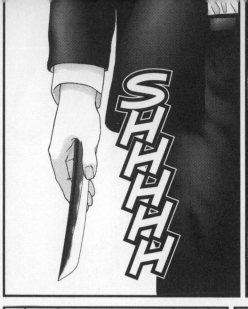
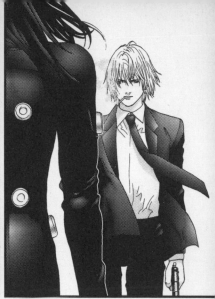

S.H.H.H.H

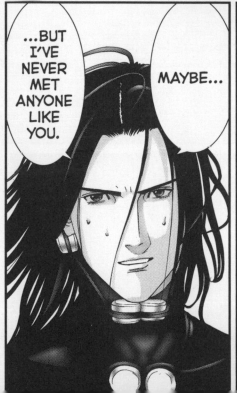

...BUT I'VE NEVER MET ANYONE LIKE YOU.

MAYBE...

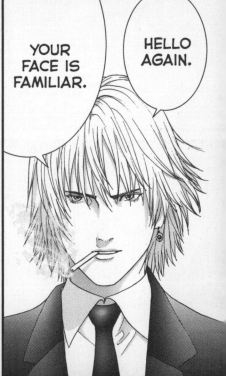

YOUR FACE IS FAMILIAR.

HELLO AGAIN.

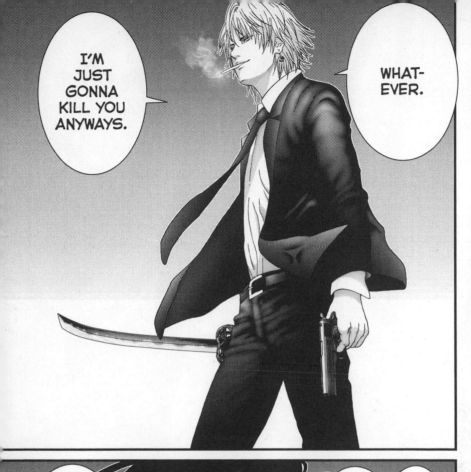

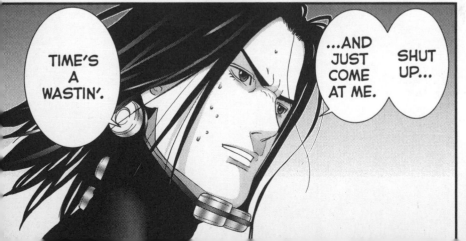

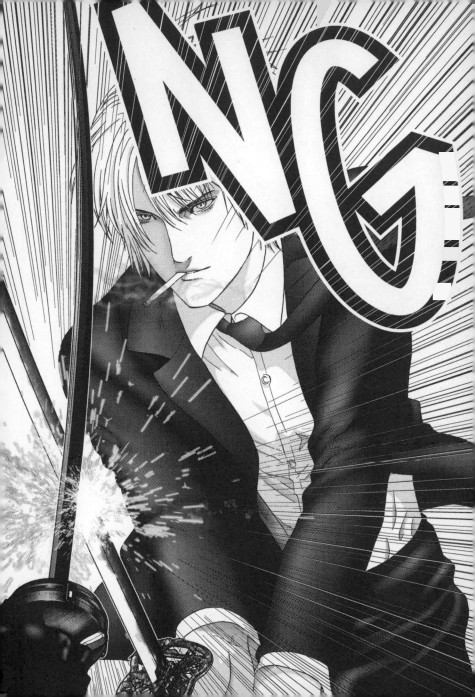

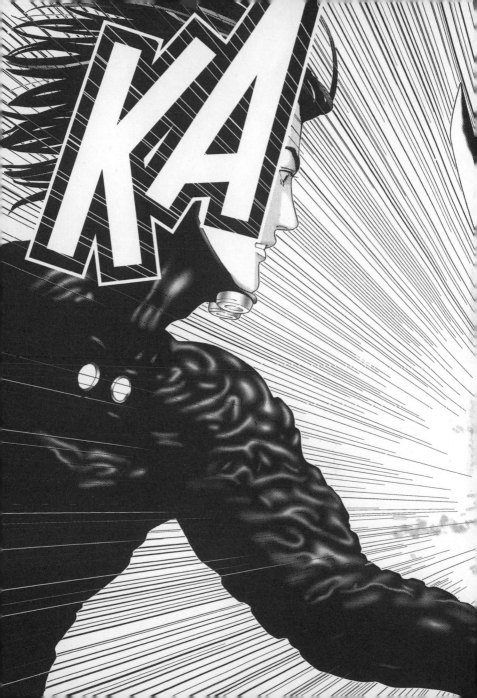

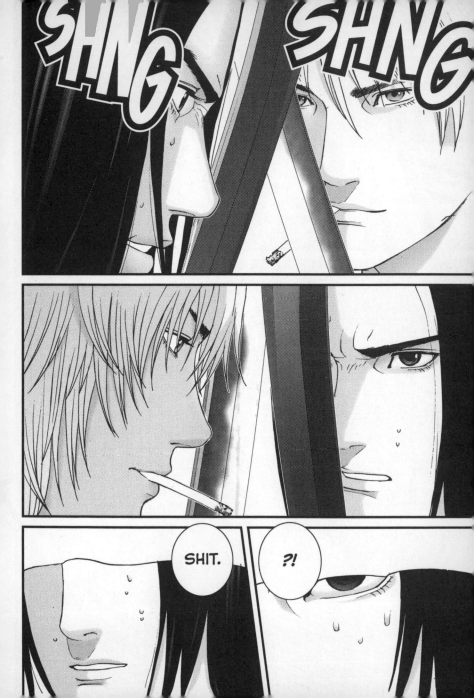

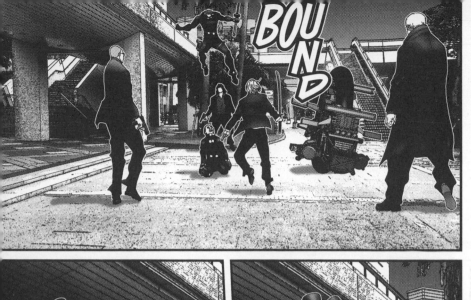

BOUND

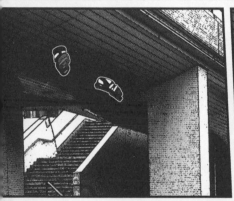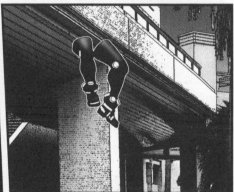

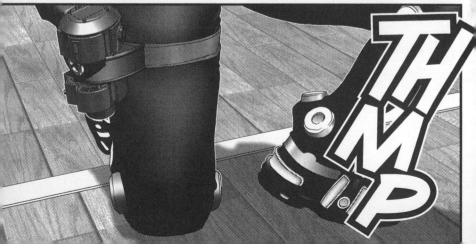

THMP

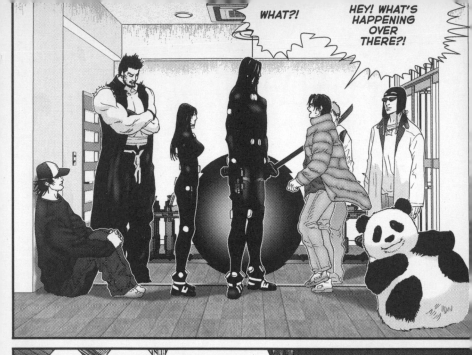

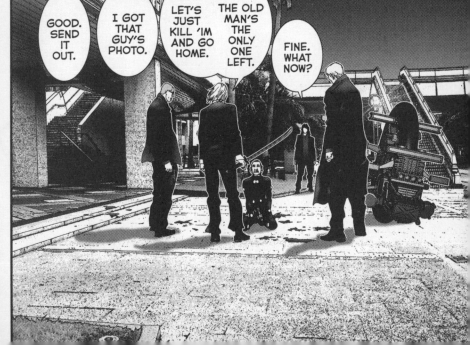

0160
THE ONLY ONE

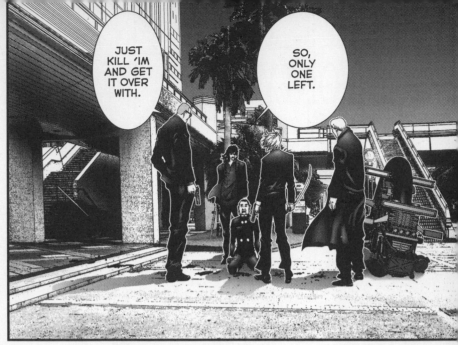

JUST KILL 'IM AND GET IT OVER WITH.

SO, ONLY ONE LEFT.

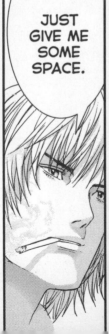

JUST GIVE ME SOME SPACE.

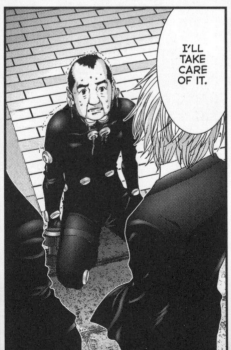

I'LL TAKE CARE OF IT.

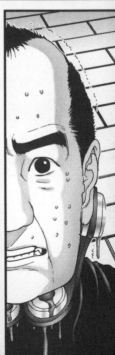

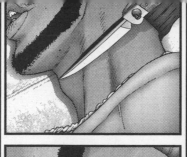
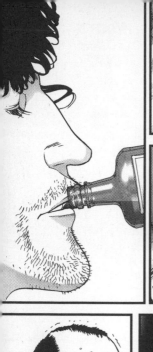
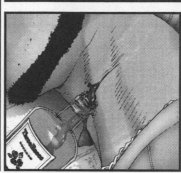
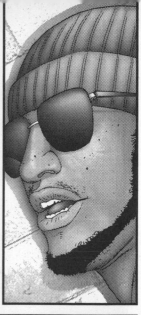
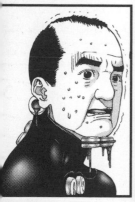
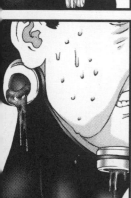
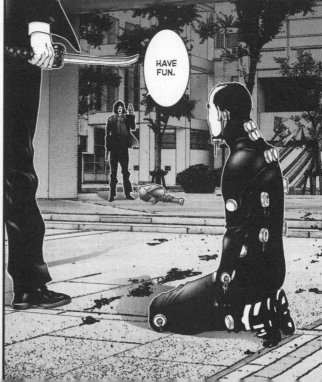

HAVE
FUN.

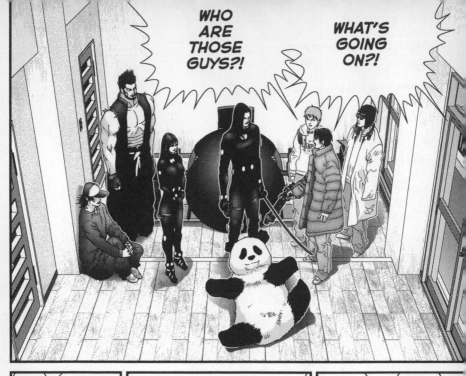

WHO ARE THOSE GUYS?!

WHAT'S GOING ON?!

OH YEAH... RIGHT.

IF THEY'RE STILL ALIVE, THEY SHOULD BE HERE ANY SECOND.

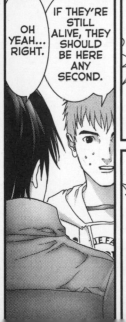

ARE YOU SURE?!

WHAT ?!

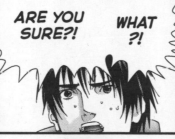

YOU BAS- TARD!

WASN'T MY JOB TO MAKE SURE.

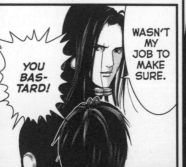

EVERY- ONE'S DEAD.

HOW SHOULD I KNOW?

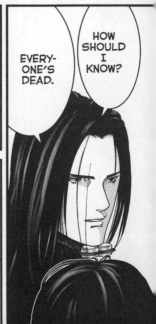

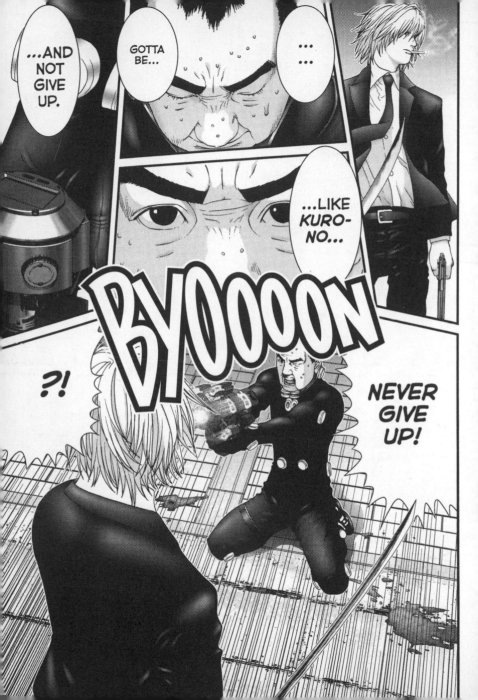

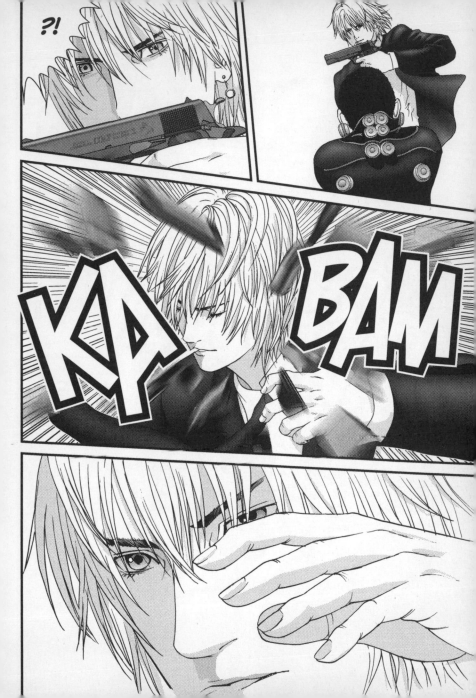

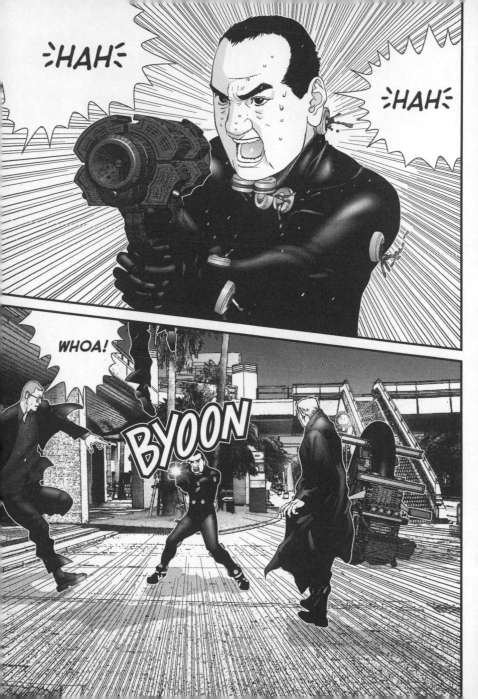

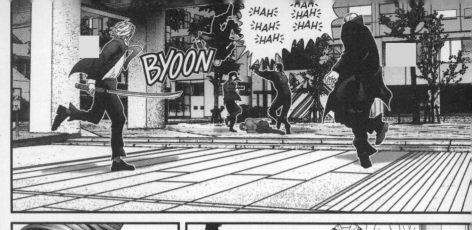

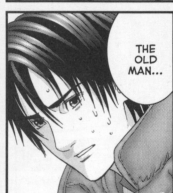

THE OLD MAN...

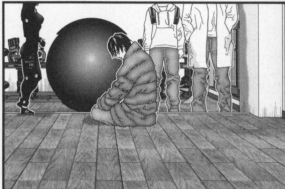

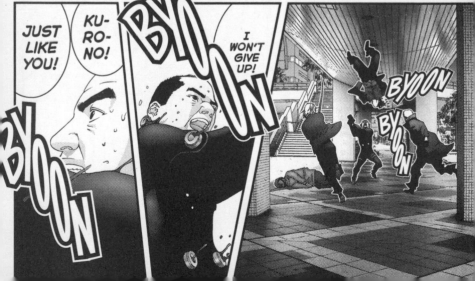

JUST LIKE YOU!

KU-RO-NO!

I WON'T GIVE UP!

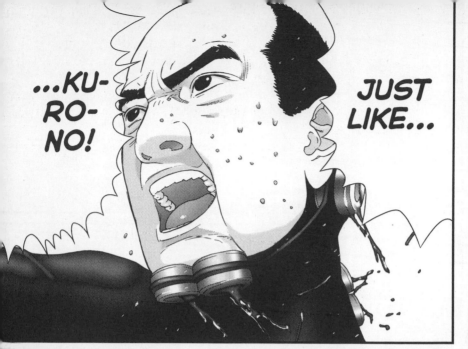

...KU-
RO-
NO!

JUST
LIKE...

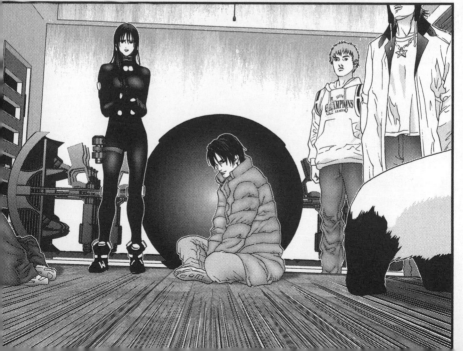

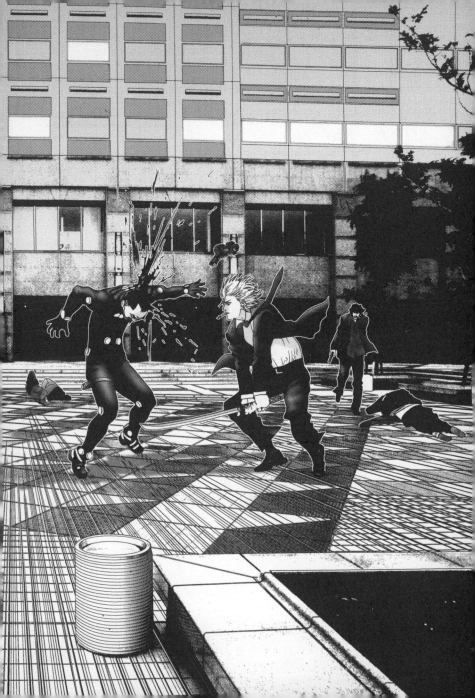

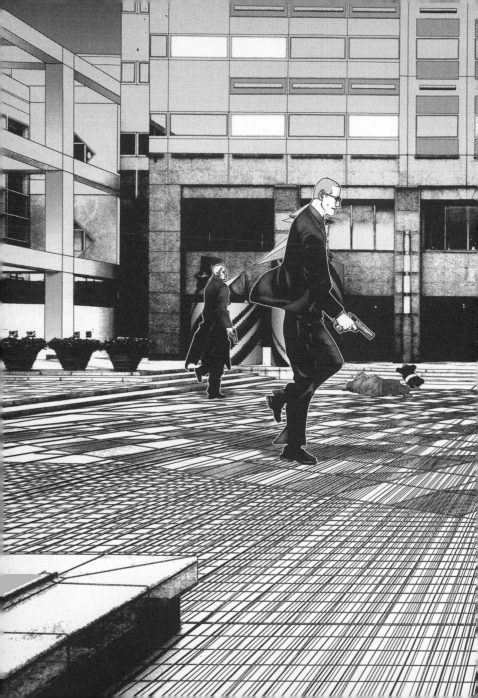

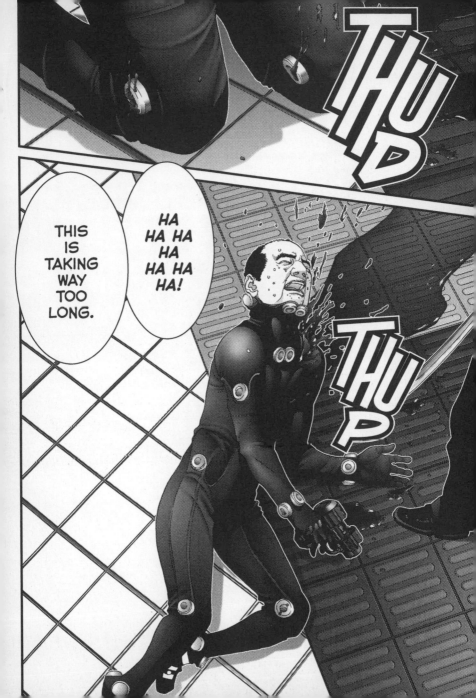

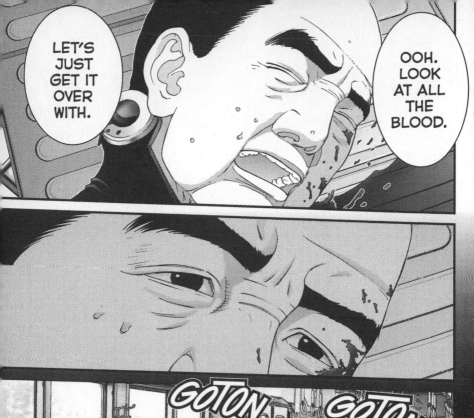

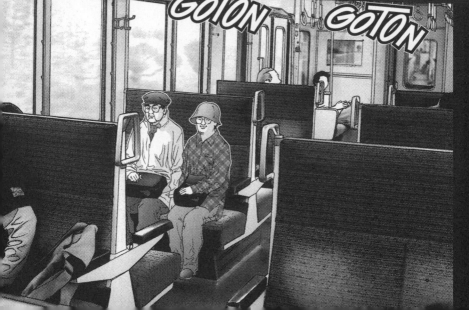

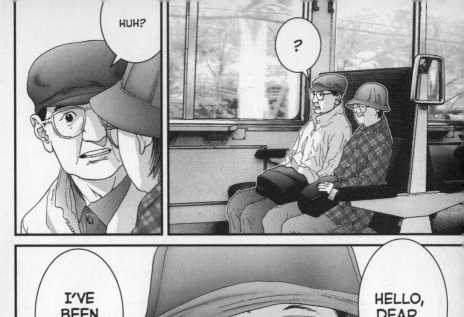

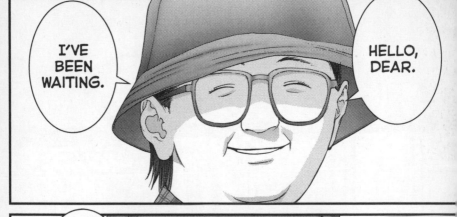

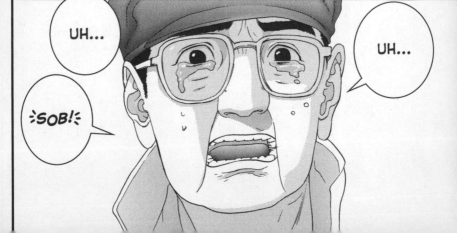

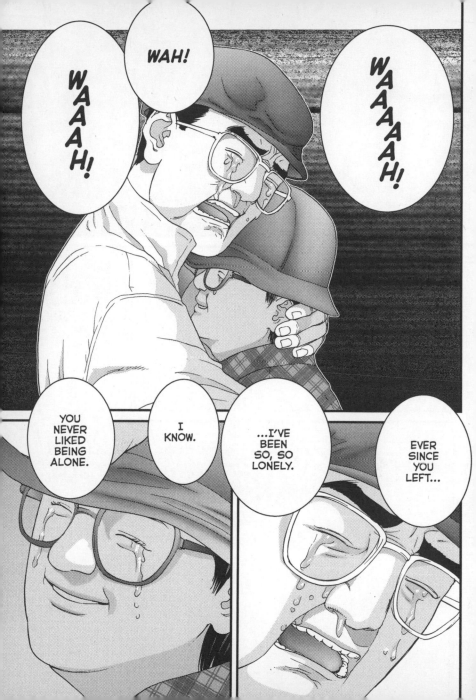

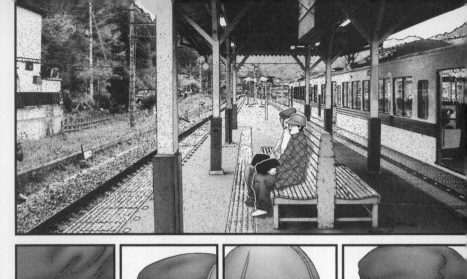

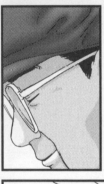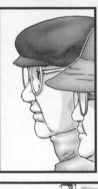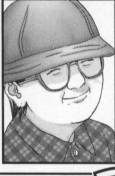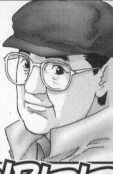

RIRIRIRIRI

RIRIRIR

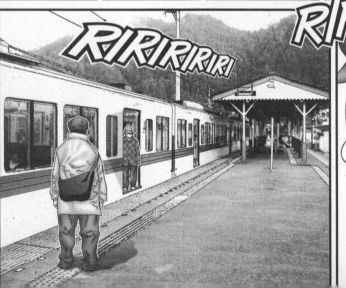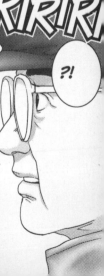

?!

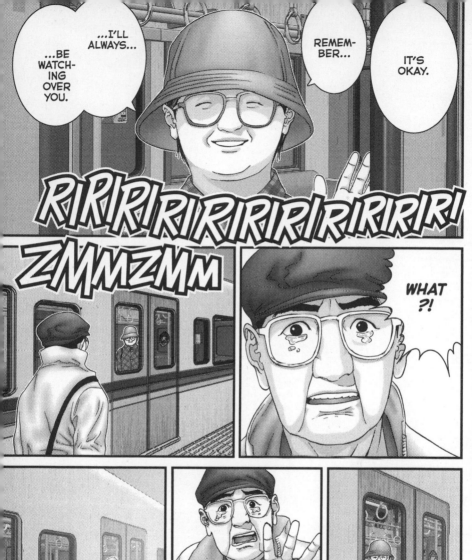

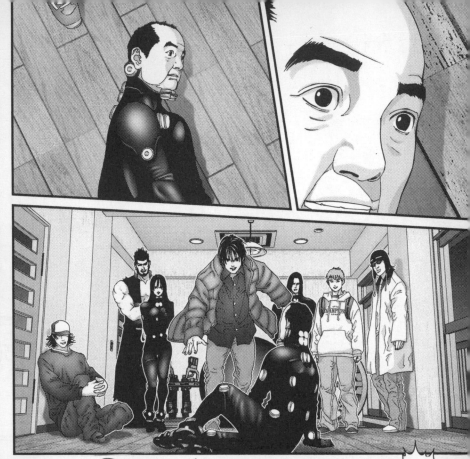

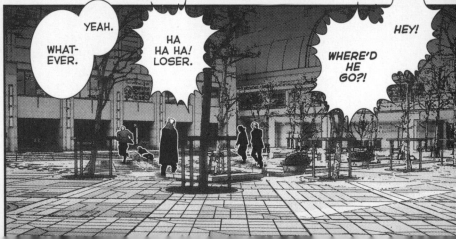

YEAH.

WHAT-
EVER.

HA
HA HA!
LOSER.

HEY!

WHERE'D
HE
GO?!

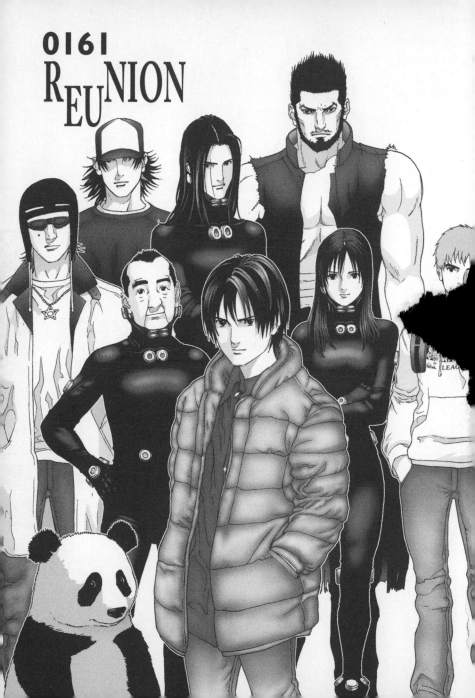

0161
REUNION

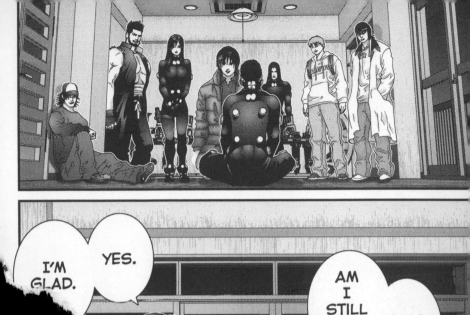

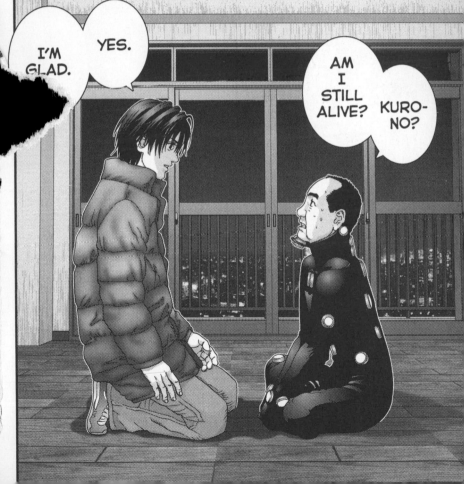

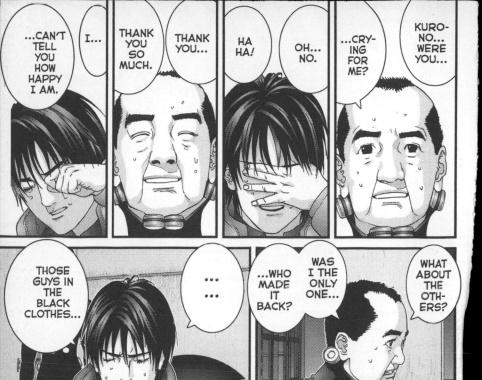

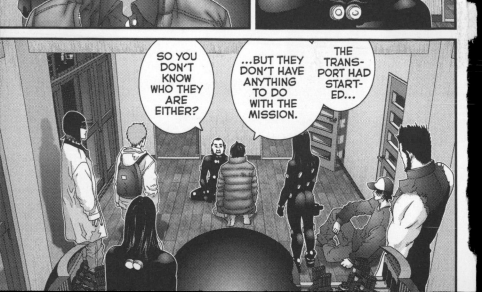

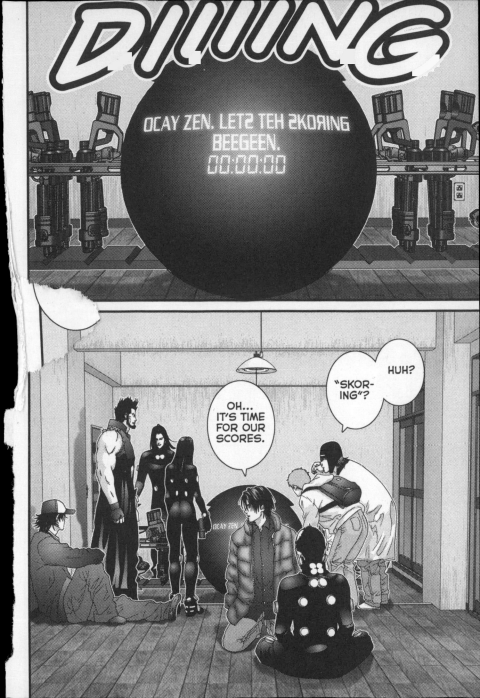

DIMWIT

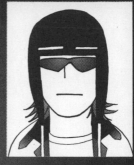

11 POINTS

TOTAL: 11POINTS
ONLY **89** LEFT
TILL YER DONE

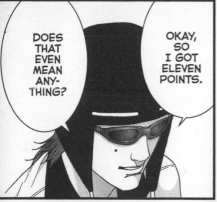

DOES THAT EVEN MEAN ANYTHING?

OKAY, SO I GOT ELEVEN POINTS.

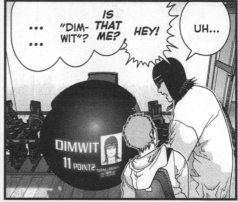

... ... "DIM-WIT"?

IS THAT ME?

HEY!

UH...

DIMWIT 11 POINTS TOTAL

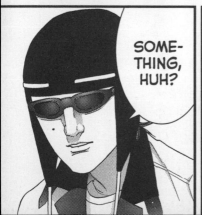

SOMETHING, HUH?

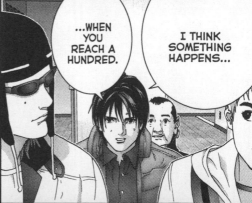

...WHEN YOU REACH A HUNDRED.

I THINK SOMETHING HAPPENS...

KURONO'S #1 FAN

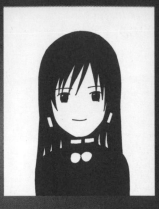

0 POINTS

TOO MUCH GAZING AT KURONO

TOTAL: 0 POINTS

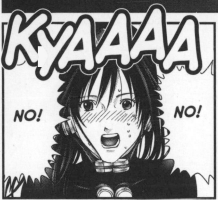

KYAAAA

NO!

NO!

WHAT?! WHAT?!

WHAT ?!

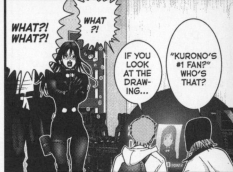

IF YOU LOOK AT THE DRAW-ING...

"KURONO'S #1 FAN?" WHO'S THAT?

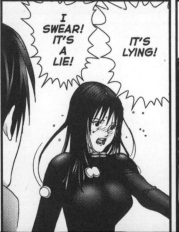

I SWEAR! IT'S A LIE!

IT'S LYING!

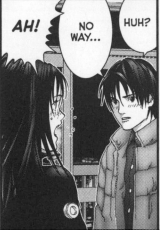

AH!

NO WAY...

HUH?

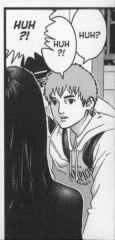

HUH ?!

HUH ?!

HUH?

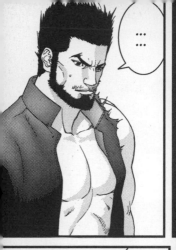

...

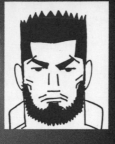

GENERAL BUMPKIN

5 POINTS

TOTAL: 5 POINTS

ONLY **95** LEFT TILL YER DONE

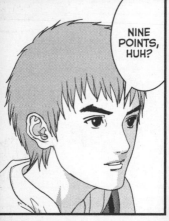

NINE POINTS, HUH?

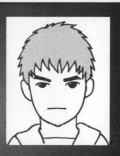

CHERRY

9 POINTS

TOTAL: 9 POINTS

ONLY **91** LEFT TILL YER DONE

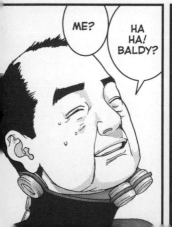

ME?

HA HA! BALDY?

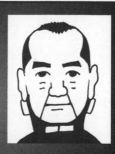

BALDY

5 POINTS

TOTAL: 5 POINTS

ONLY **95** LEFT TILL YER DONE

HOI HOI

0 POINTZ

ZUMZ GOOD MOTOVAZION, BUT GLOMMED ON TO IZUMI TOO MUCH

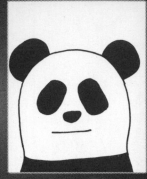

TOTAL: 0 POINTZ

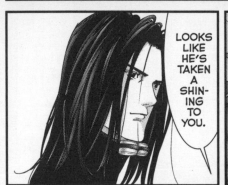

LOOKS LIKE HE'S TAKEN A SHINING TO YOU.

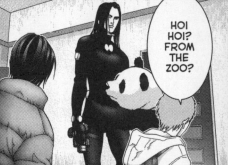

HOI HOI? FROM THE ZOO?

...

"TOO MUCH ACTING COOL"?

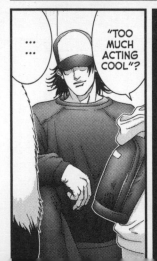

INABA

0 POINTZ

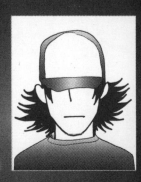

TOO MUCH ACTING COOL NO ЯEAL HELP

TOTAL: 0 POINTZ

IZUMI
16POINTS

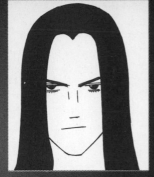

TOTAL: 16POINTS
ONLY **84** LEFT
TILL YER DONE

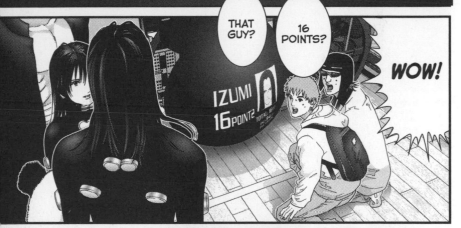

THAT GUY?

16 POINTS?

IZUMI 16POINTS

WOW!

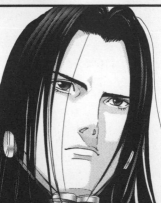

YOU ALL JUST GOT LUCKY.

OF COURSE. DON'T TRY TO LUMP ME IN WITH YOU.

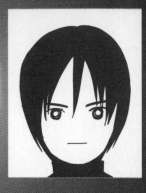

KURONO
58POINTS

TOTAL: 58POINTS
ONLY **42** LEFT
TILL YER DONE

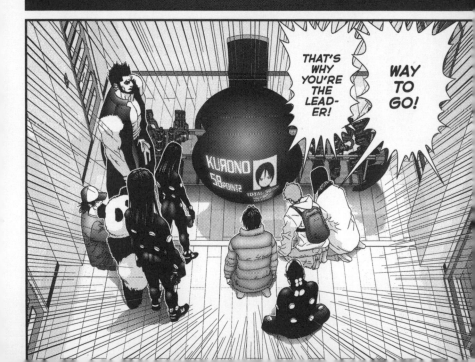

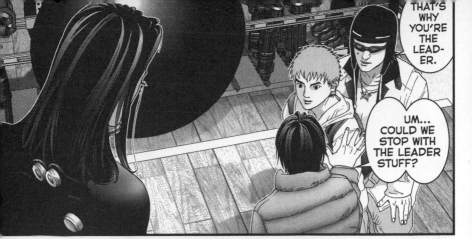

THAT'S WHY YOU'RE THE LEADER.

UM... COULD WE STOP WITH THE LEADER STUFF?

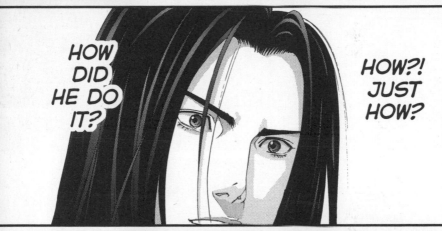

HOW DID HE DO IT?

HOW?! JUST HOW?

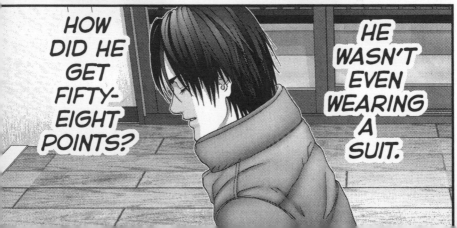

HOW DID HE GET FIFTY-EIGHT POINTS?

HE WASN'T EVEN WEARING A SUIT.

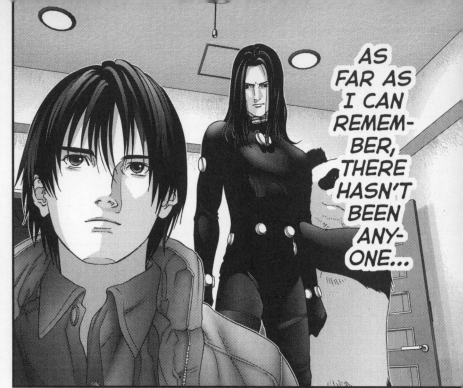

AS FAR AS I CAN REMEMBER, THERE HASN'T BEEN ANYONE...

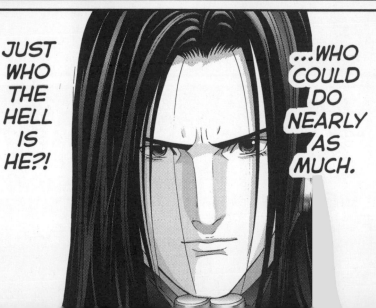

JUST WHO THE HELL IS HE?!

...WHO COULD DO NEARLY AS MUCH.

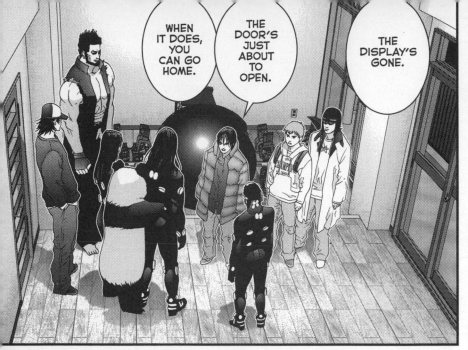

WHEN IT DOES, YOU CAN GO HOME.

THE DOOR'S JUST ABOUT TO OPEN.

THE DISPLAY'S GONE.

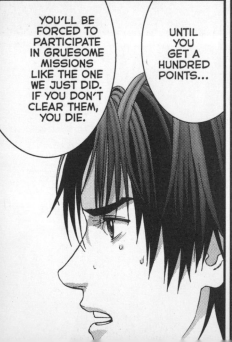

YOU'LL BE FORCED TO PARTICIPATE IN GRUESOME MISSIONS LIKE THE ONE WE JUST DID. IF YOU DON'T CLEAR THEM, YOU DIE.

UNTIL YOU GET A HUNDRED POINTS...

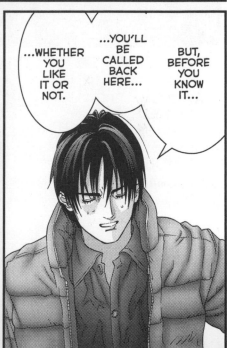

...WHETHER YOU LIKE IT OR NOT.

...YOU'LL BE CALLED BACK HERE...

BUT, BEFORE YOU KNOW IT...

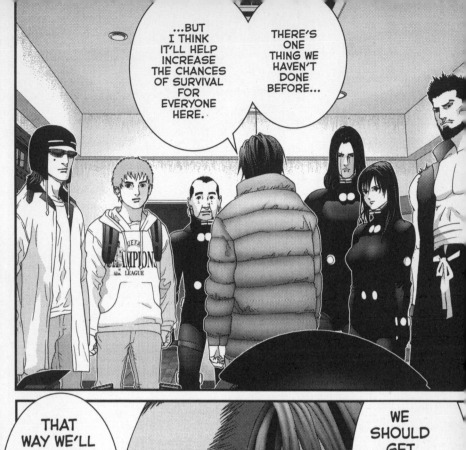

...BUT I THINK IT'LL HELP INCREASE THE CHANCES OF SURVIVAL FOR EVERYONE HERE.

THERE'S ONE THING WE HAVEN'T DONE BEFORE...

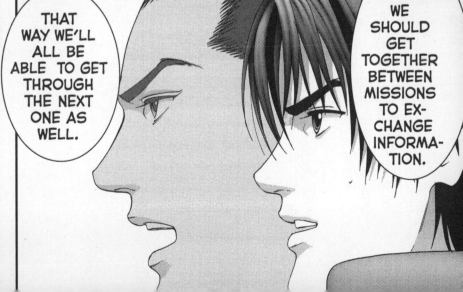

THAT WAY WE'LL ALL BE ABLE TO GET THROUGH THE NEXT ONE AS WELL.

WE SHOULD GET TOGETHER BETWEEN MISSIONS TO EX-CHANGE INFORMA-TION.

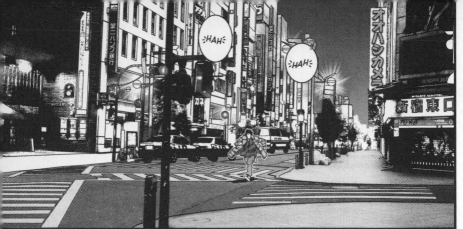

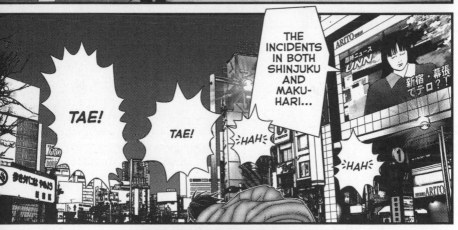

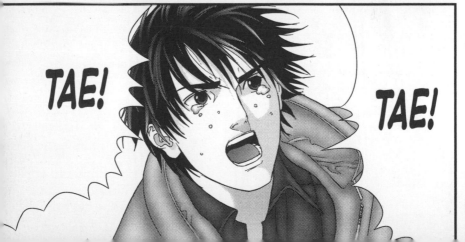

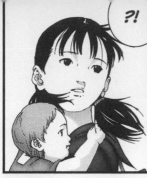
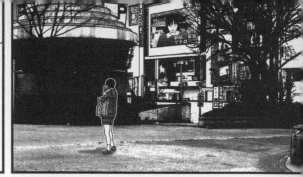
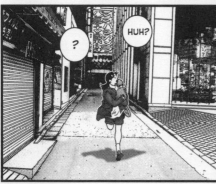
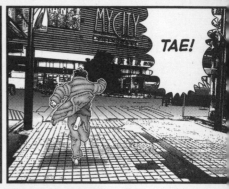
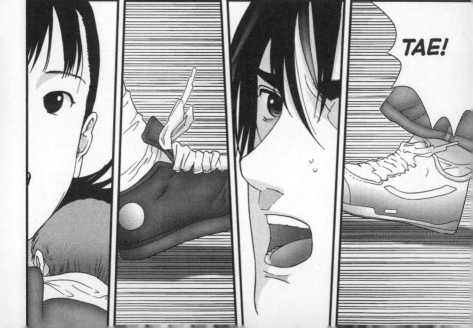

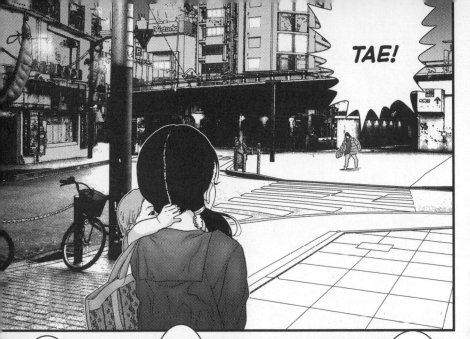

TAE!

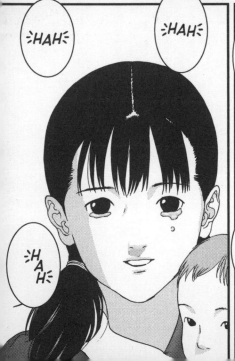

≍HAH≍

≍HAH≍

≍H A H≍

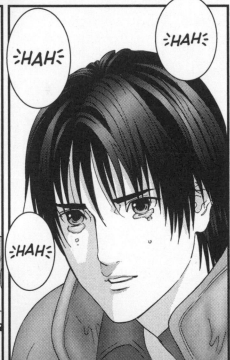

≍HAH≍

≍HAH≍

≍HAH≍

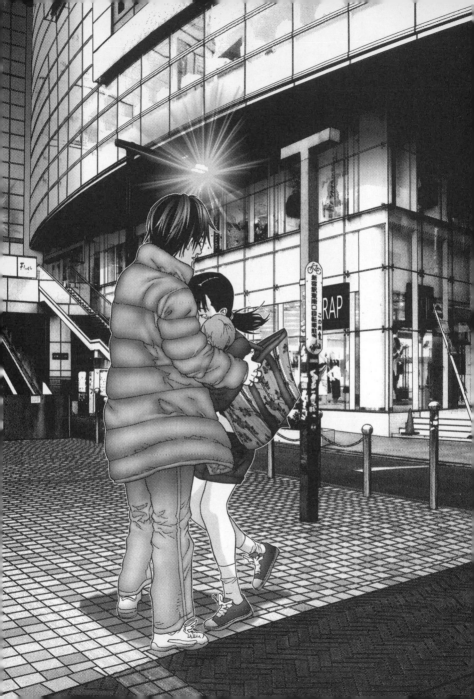

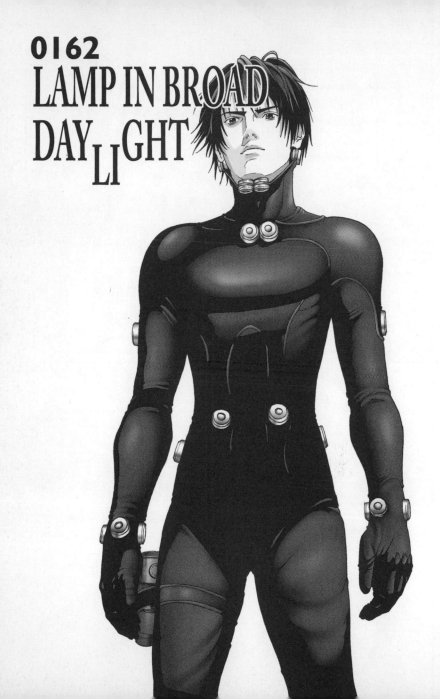

0162
LAMP IN BROAD
DAY LIGHT

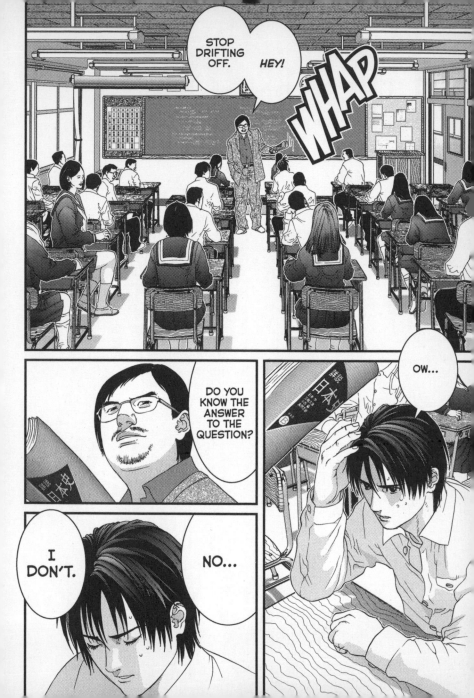

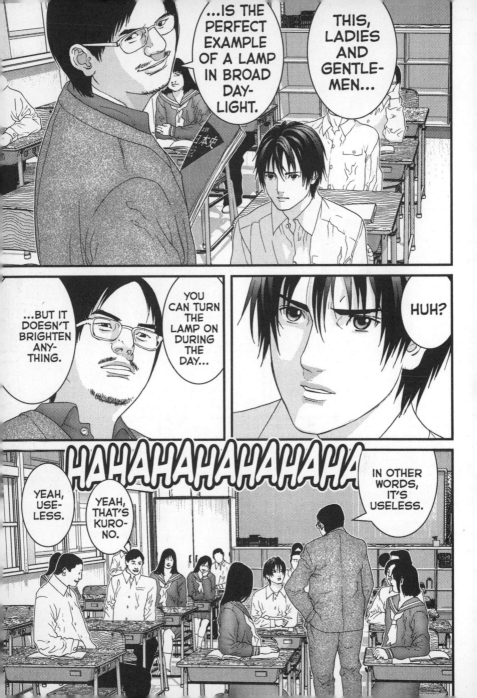

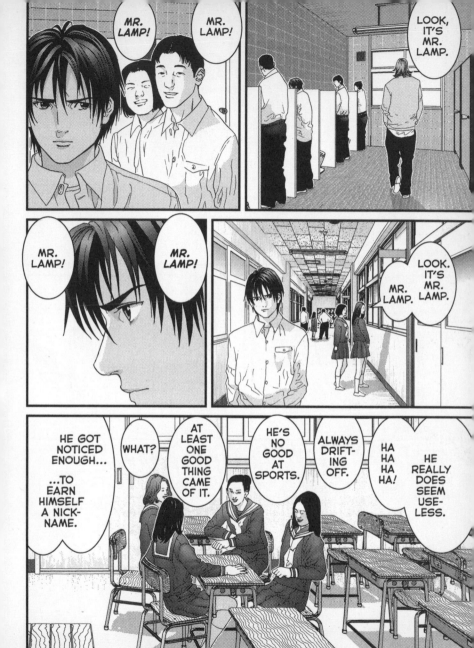

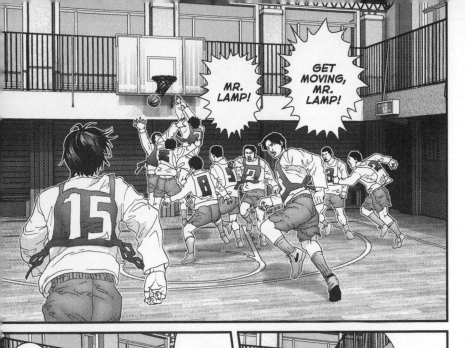

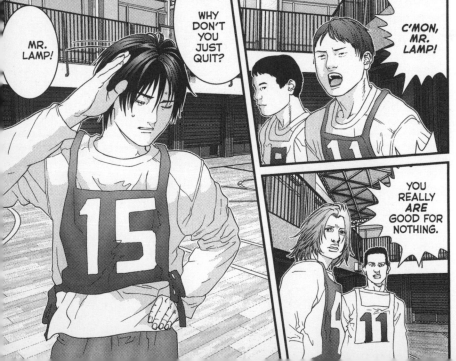

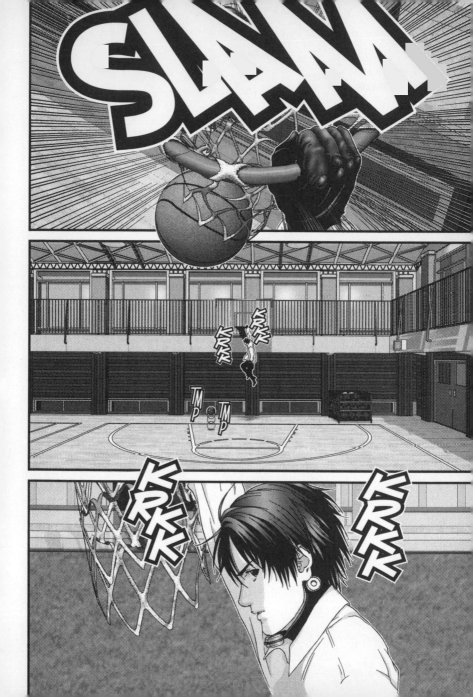

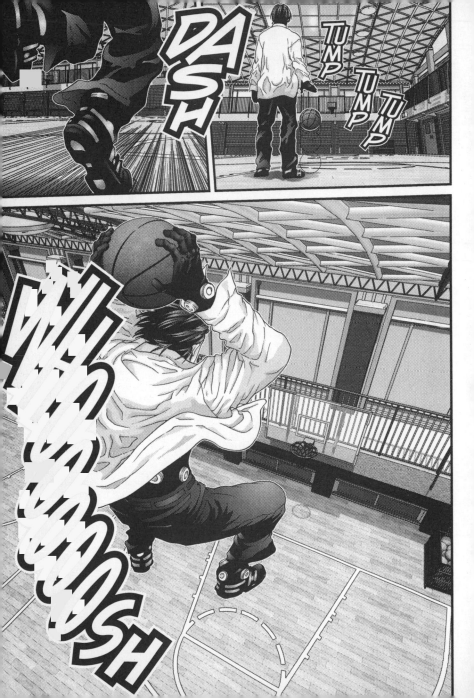

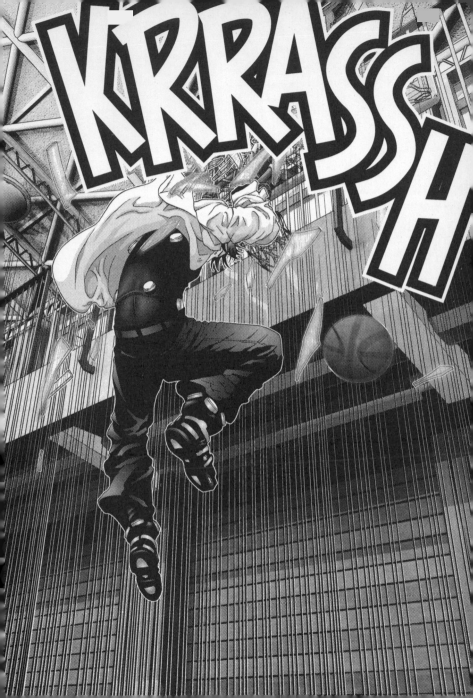

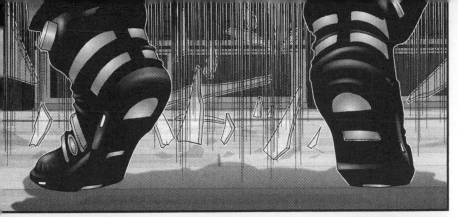

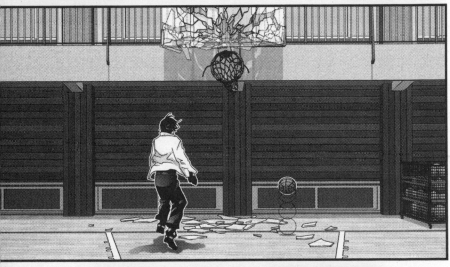

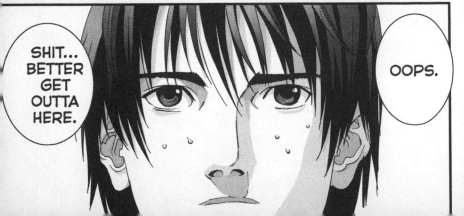

SHIT... BETTER GET OUTTA HERE.

OOPS.

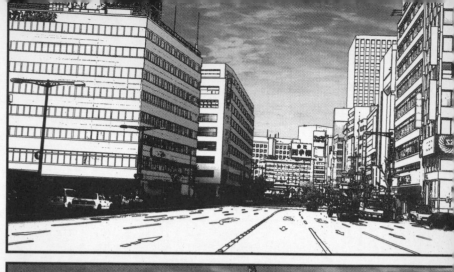

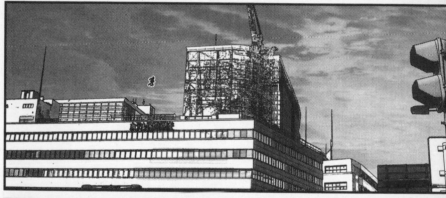

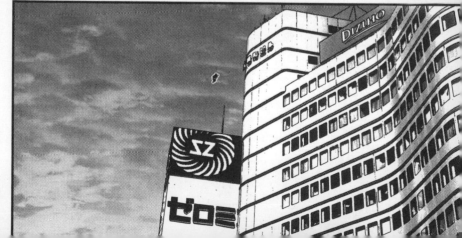

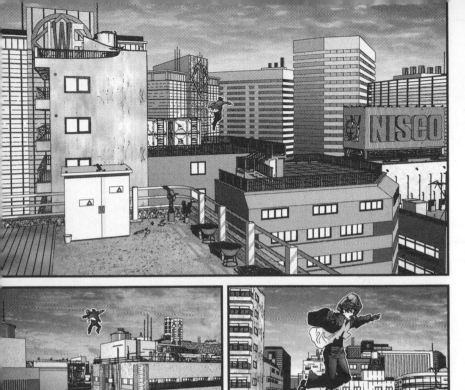

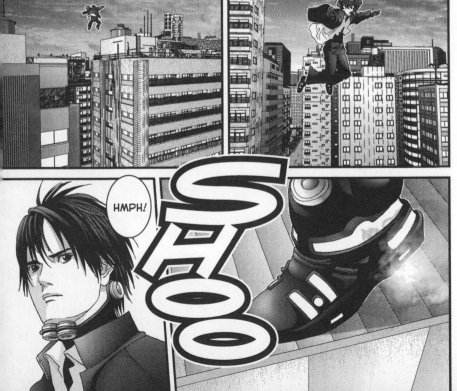

HMPH!

SHOO

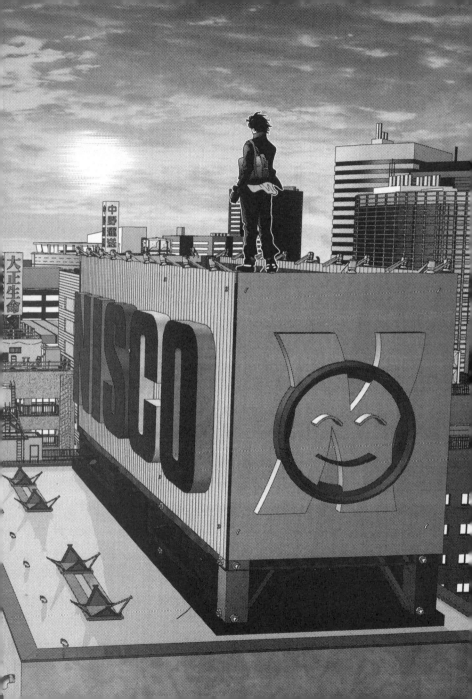

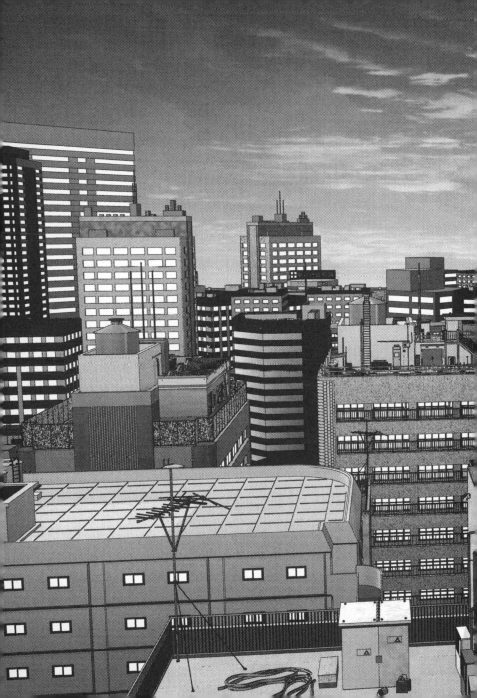

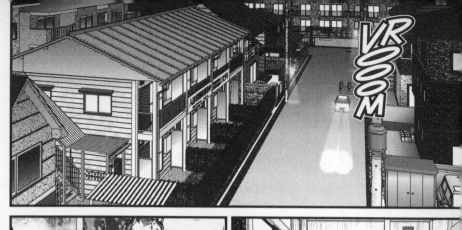

VROOM

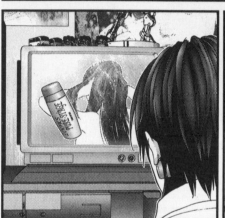

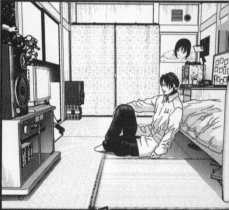

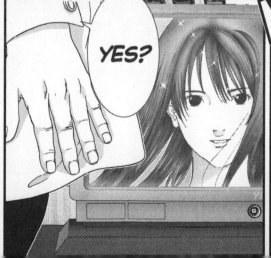

YES?

NOK NOK

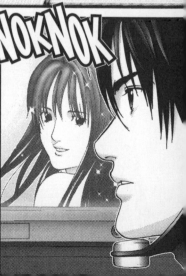

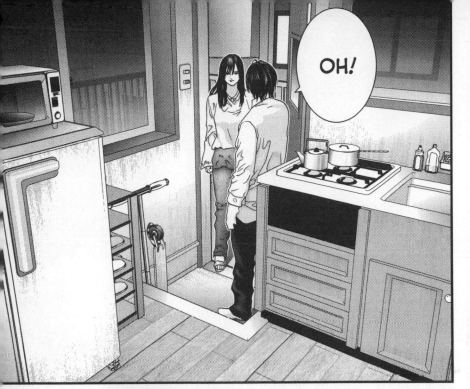

OH!

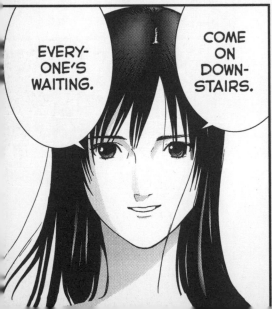

EVERY-ONE'S WAITING.

COME ON DOWN-STAIRS.

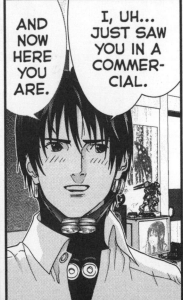

AND NOW HERE YOU ARE.

I, UH... JUST SAW YOU IN A COMMER-CIAL.

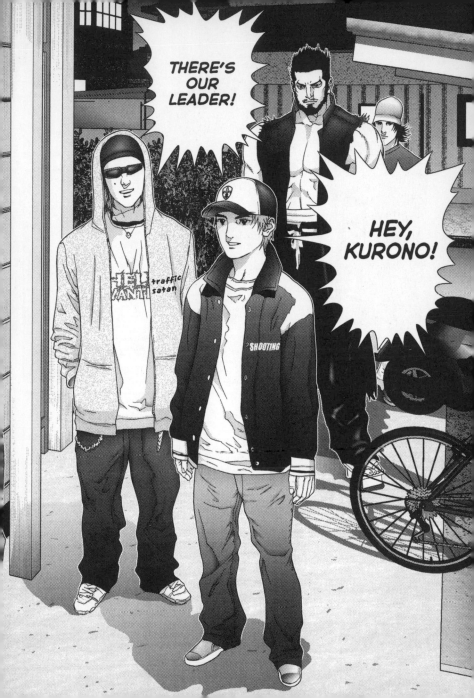

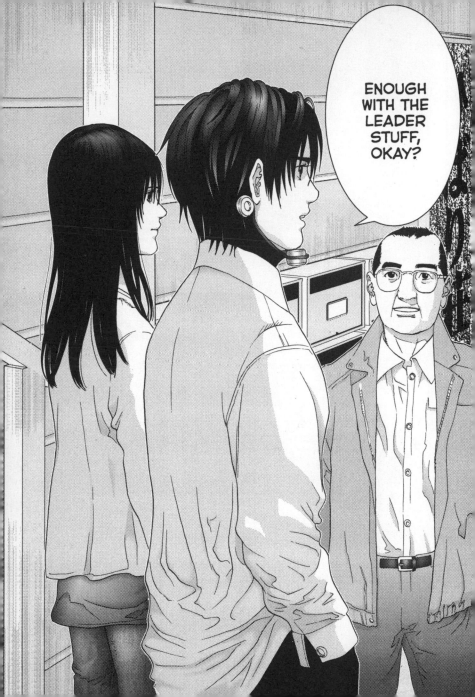

IF HUMANS ARE SPLIT INTO THOSE WHO ARE ALIGNED WITH GOD AND THOSE WHO ARE ALIGNED WITH THE DEVIL, WHICH AM I?

I USED TO THINK A LOT ABOUT IT AS A KID.

0163 SEMINAR

GOOD OR EVIL. WHICH AM I?

AH!

THERE'S NO CUT, RIGHT?

I TOLD YOU, IT'S OKAY.

I MUST HAVE CUT YOU.

I'M SO SORRY. MY HAND SLIPPED.

THESE HEAD-ACHES ARE KILLIN' ME.

OH, MAN.

THUD

SKREEEEECH

SKRR

A-ARE YOU OKAY?

YEAH. I'M OKAY.

WHAT... HEY.

SHFF

KG HAK

...BUT I'M NOT.

IT'S LIKE I'M ME...

WAS I JUST HIT BY A CAR?

JUST WHAT THE HELL IS GOIN' ON?

CAN I BOTHER YOU FOR A MINUTE?

SELF-DISCOVERY SEMINAR

YOU WANT TO JOIN ME FOR A LITTLE WHILE?

I COULD SEE IT JUST BY LOOKING IN YOUR EYES.

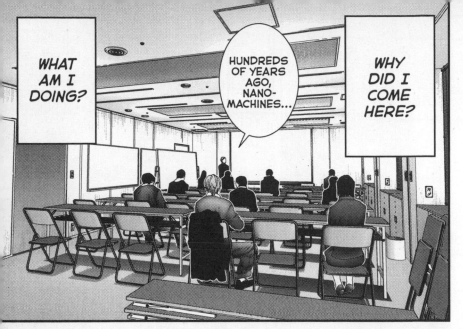

WHAT AM I DOING?

HUNDREDS OF YEARS AGO, NANO-MACHINES...

WHY DID I COME HERE?

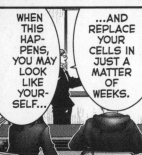

WHEN THIS HAPPENS, YOU MAY LOOK LIKE YOURSELF...

...AND REPLACE YOUR CELLS IN JUST A MATTER OF WEEKS.

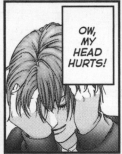

OW, MY HEAD HURTS!

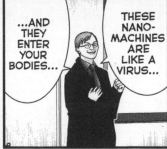

...AND THEY ENTER YOUR BODIES...

THESE NANO-MACHINES ARE LIKE A VIRUS...

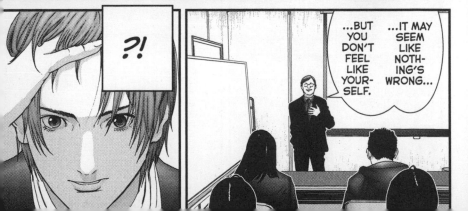

?!

...BUT YOU DON'T FEEL LIKE YOURSELF.

...IT MAY SEEM LIKE NOTHING'S WRONG...

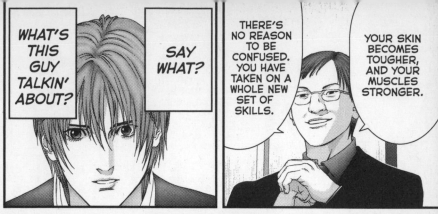

WHAT'S THIS GUY TALKIN' ABOUT?

SAY WHAT?

THERE'S NO REASON TO BE CONFUSED. YOU HAVE TAKEN ON A WHOLE NEW SET OF SKILLS.

YOUR SKIN BECOMES TOUGHER, AND YOUR MUSCLES STRONGER.

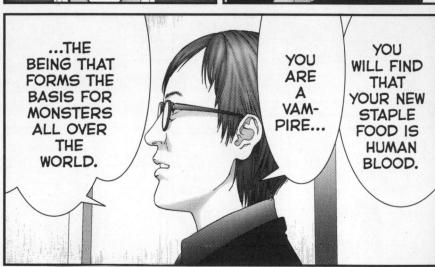

...THE BEING THAT FORMS THE BASIS FOR MONSTERS ALL OVER THE WORLD.

YOU ARE A VAMPIRE...

YOU WILL FIND THAT YOUR NEW STAPLE FOOD IS HUMAN BLOOD.

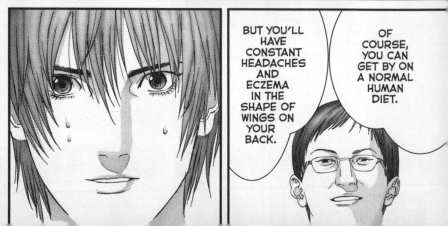

BUT YOU'LL HAVE CONSTANT HEADACHES AND ECZEMA IN THE SHAPE OF WINGS ON YOUR BACK.

OF COURSE, YOU CAN GET BY ON A NORMAL HUMAN DIET.

...BUT A GROUP THAT WEARS BLACK, MECHANICAL OUTFITS.

YOU HAVE ENEMIES. IT'S NOT THE CROSS OR A PRIEST...

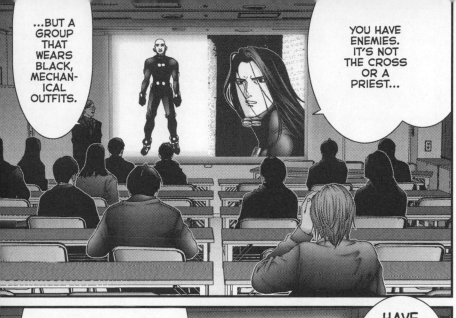

...AND USE YOUR STRENGTH TO WIPE OUT YOUR SWORN ENEMIES.

FEED ON THEM...

HAVE PRIDE IN BEING SOMETHING DIFFERENT THAN HUMAN.

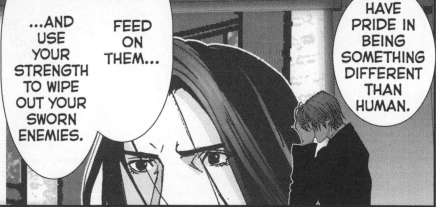

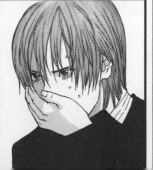

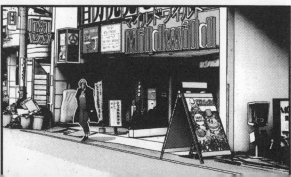

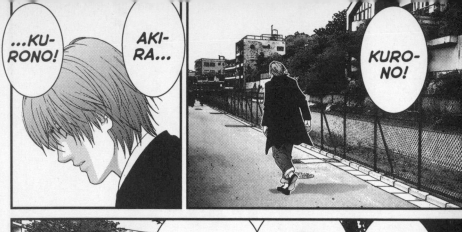

...KU-RONO!

AKI-RA...

KURO-NO!

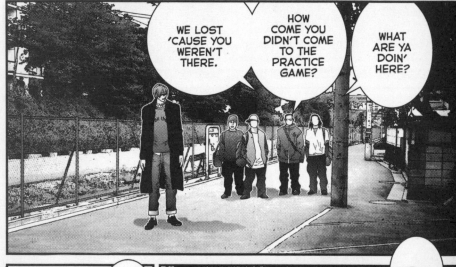

WE LOST 'CAUSE YOU WEREN'T THERE.

HOW COME YOU DIDN'T COME TO THE PRACTICE GAME?

WHAT ARE YA DOIN' HERE?

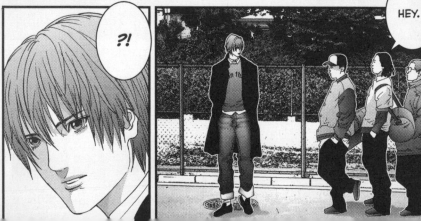

?!

HEY.

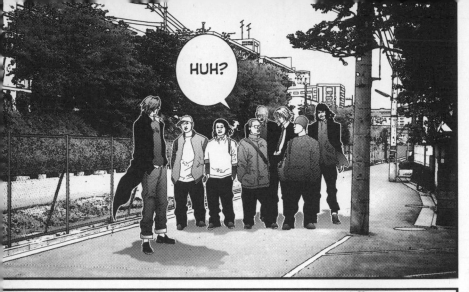

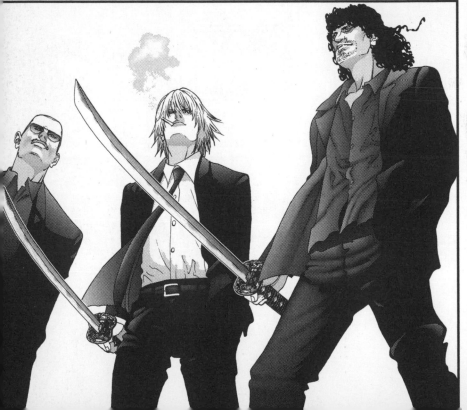

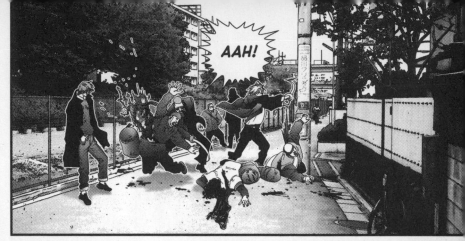

AAH!

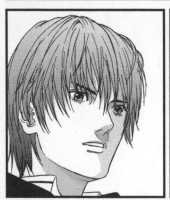

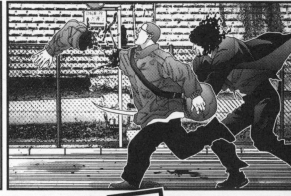

FWOP

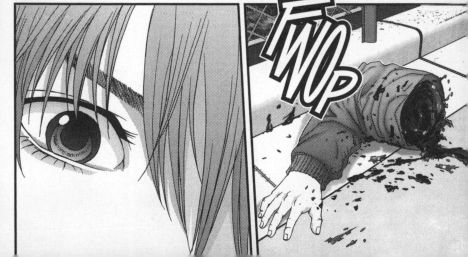

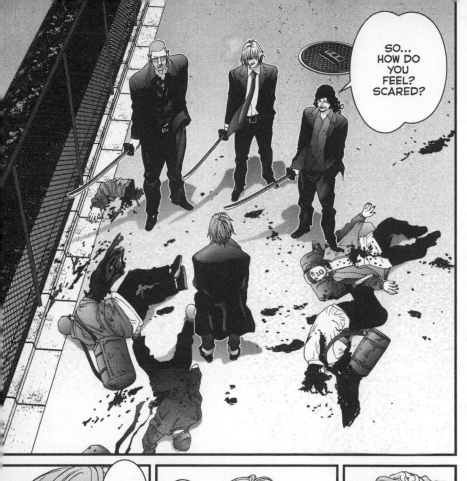

SO...
HOW DO
YOU
FEEL?
SCARED?

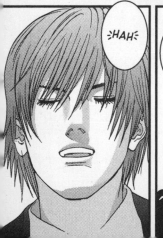

=HAH=

=HAH=

=HAH=

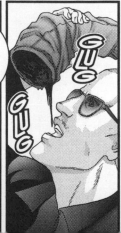

GUG

GUG

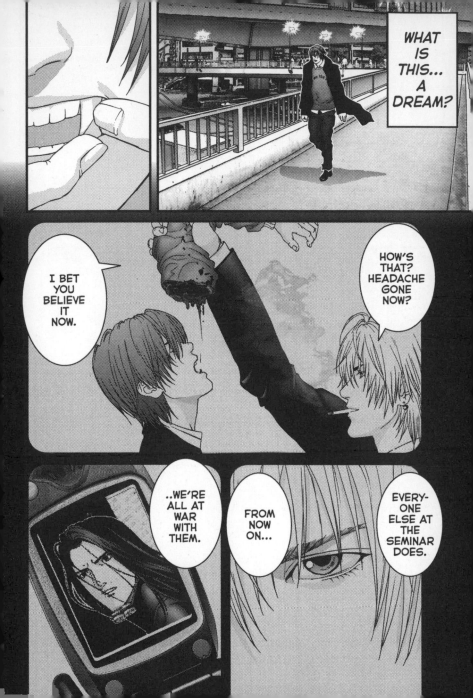

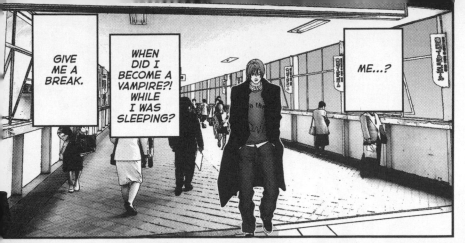

GIVE ME A BREAK.

WHEN DID I BECOME A VAMPIRE?! WHILE I WAS SLEEPING?

ME...?

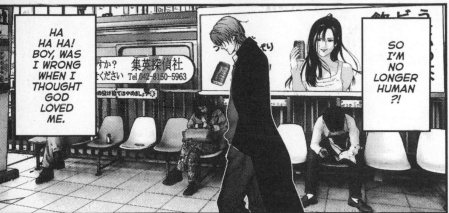

HA HA HA! BOY, WAS I WRONG WHEN I THOUGHT GOD LOVED ME.

SO I'M NO LONGER HUMAN?!

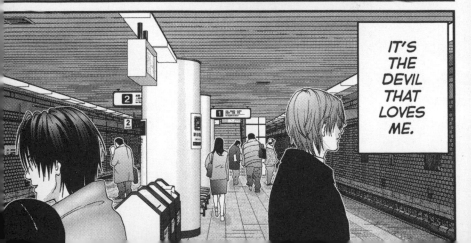

IT'S THE DEVIL THAT LOVES ME.

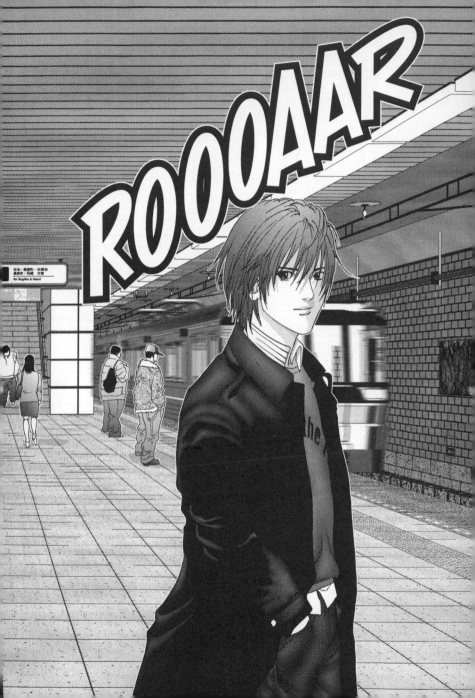

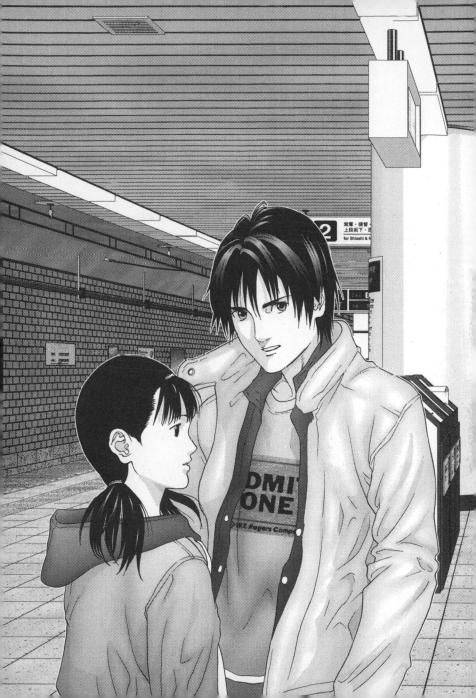

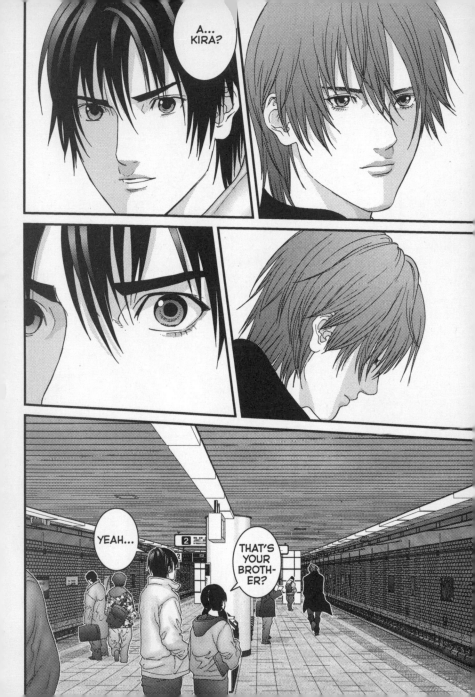

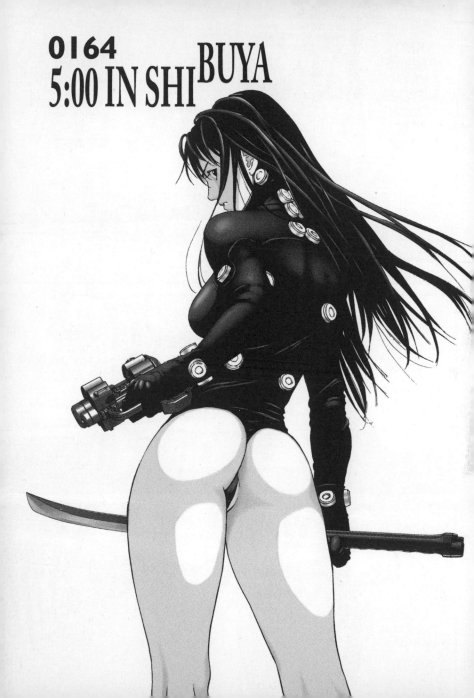

0164
5:00 IN SHI^{BUYA}

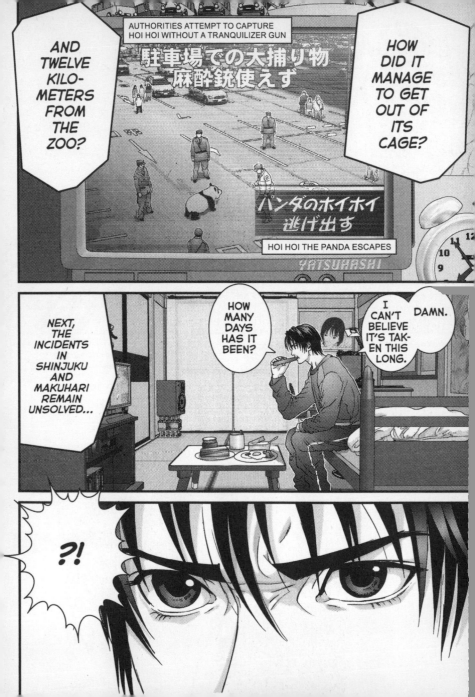

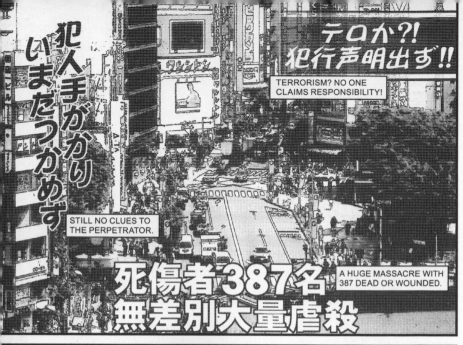

テロか?!
犯行声明出ず!!

TERRORISM? NO ONE CLAIMS RESPONSIBILITY!

犯人手がかりいまだつかめず

STILL NO CLUES TO THE PERPETRATOR.

死傷者387名
無差別大量虐殺

A HUGE MASSACRE WITH 387 DEAD OR WOUNDED.

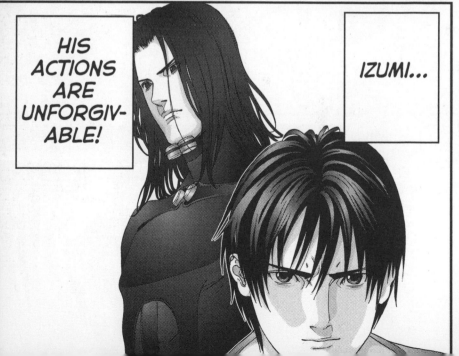

HIS ACTIONS ARE UNFORGIV-ABLE!

IZUMI...

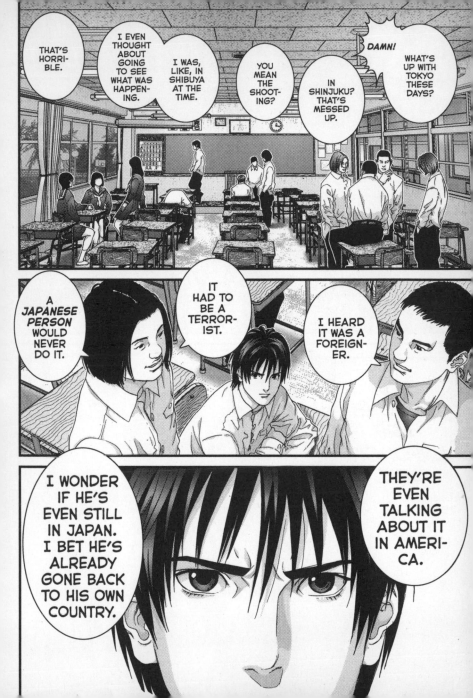

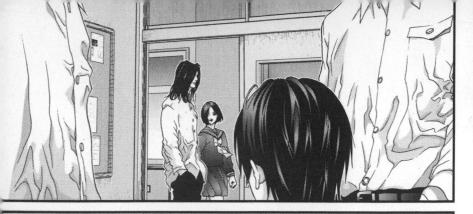

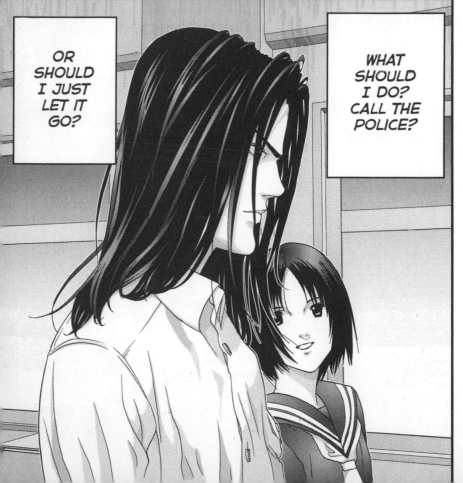

OR SHOULD I JUST LET IT GO?

WHAT SHOULD I DO? CALL THE POLICE?

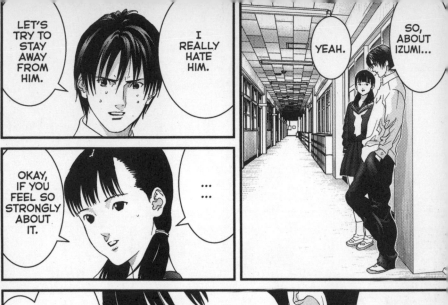

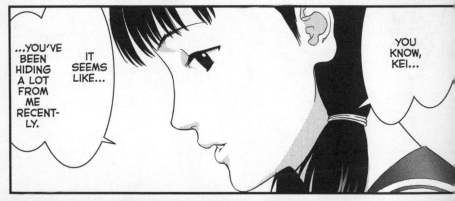

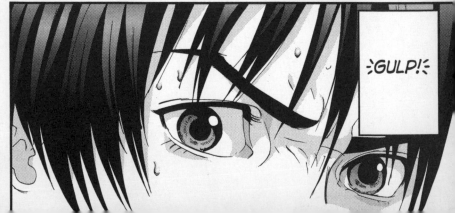

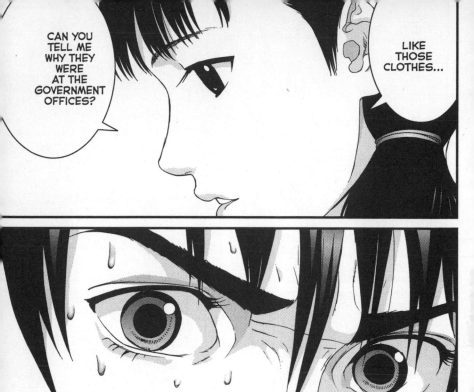

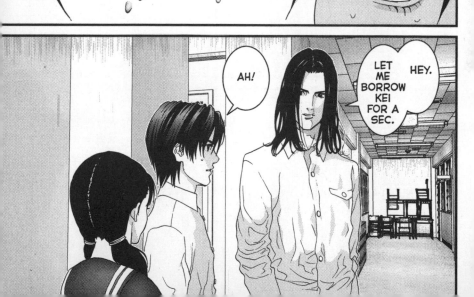

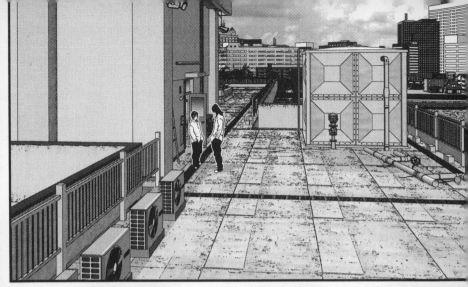

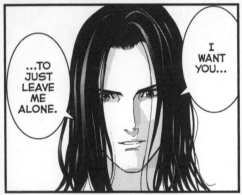

...TO JUST LEAVE ME ALONE.

I WANT YOU...

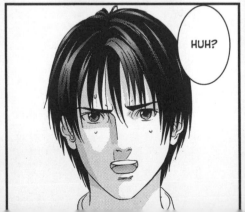

HUH?

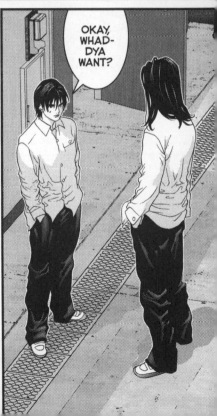

OKAY, WHAD-DYA WANT?

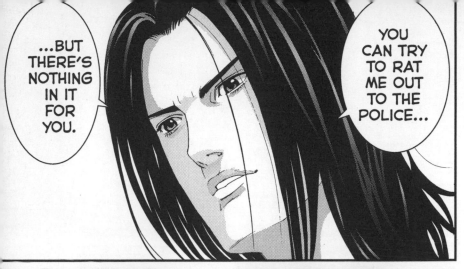

...BUT THERE'S NOTHING IN IT FOR YOU.

YOU CAN TRY TO RAT ME OUT TO THE POLICE...

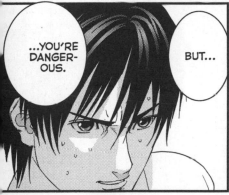

...YOU'RE DANGEROUS.

BUT...

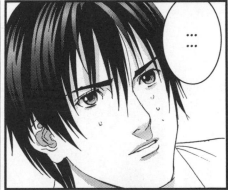

...

...

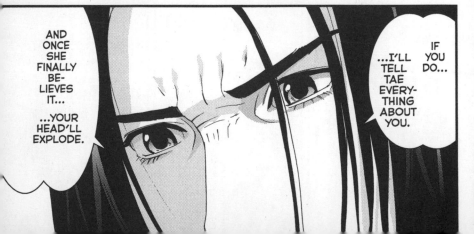

AND ONCE SHE FINALLY BELIEVES IT...

...YOUR HEAD'LL EXPLODE.

...I'LL TELL TAE EVERYTHING ABOUT YOU.

IF YOU DO...

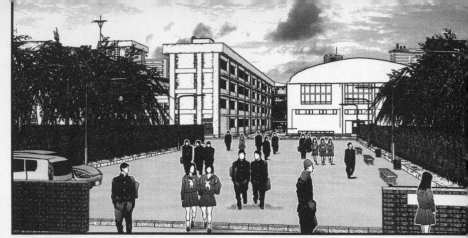

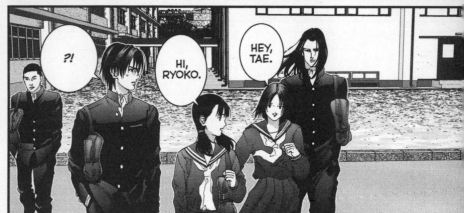

?!

HI, RYOKO.

HEY, TAE.

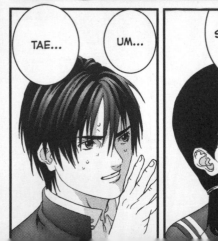

TAE...

UM...

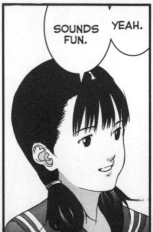

SOUNDS FUN.

YEAH.

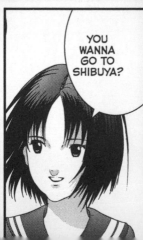

YOU WANNA GO TO SHIBUYA?

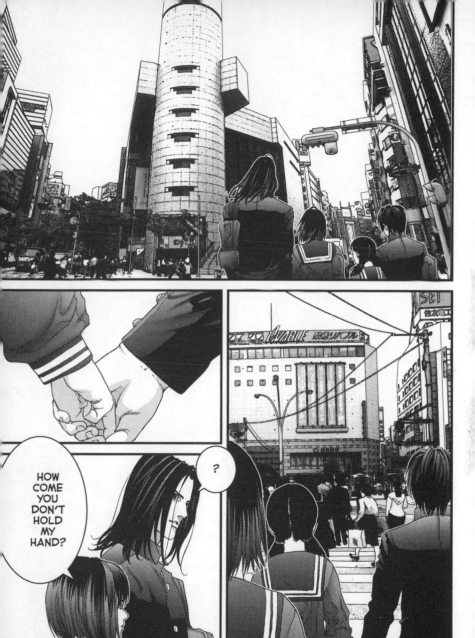

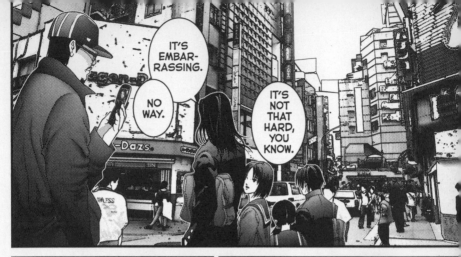

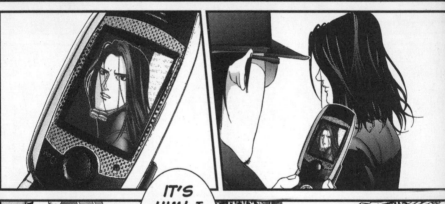

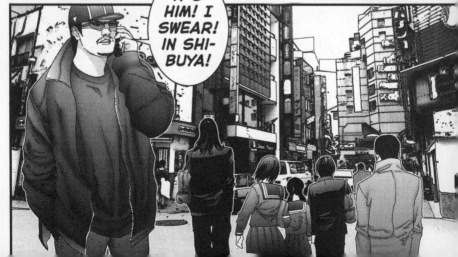

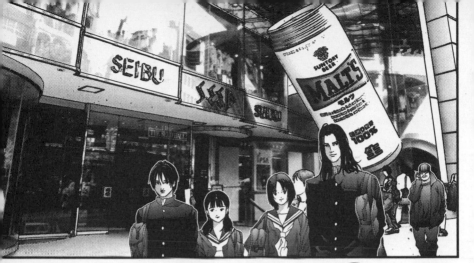

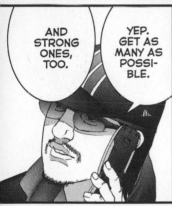

AND STRONG ONES, TOO.

YEP. GET AS MANY AS POSSIBLE.

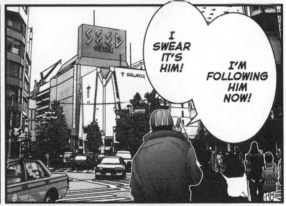

I SWEAR IT'S HIM!

I'M FOLLOWING HIM NOW!

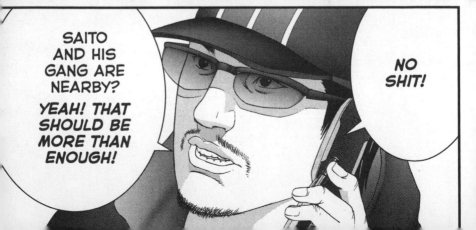

SAITO AND HIS GANG ARE NEARBY?

YEAH! THAT SHOULD BE MORE THAN ENOUGH!

NO SHIT!

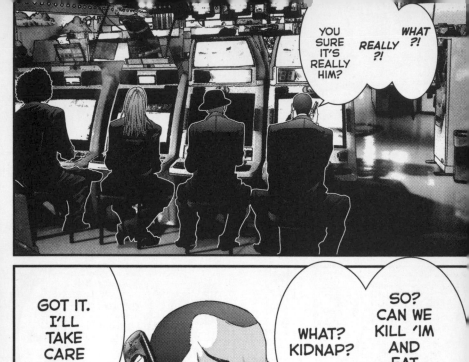

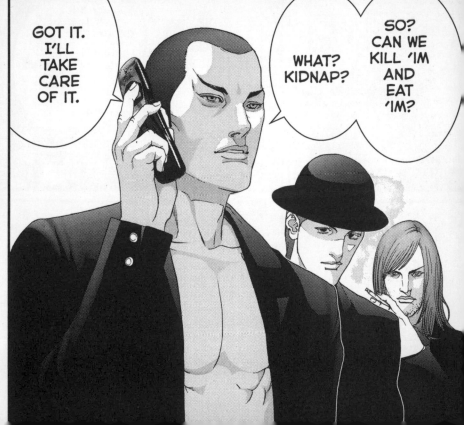

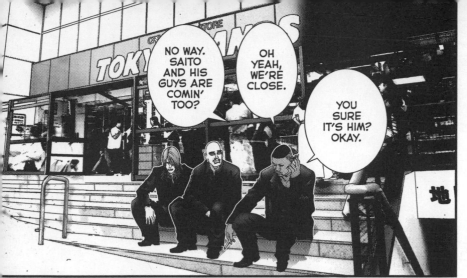

NO WAY. SAITO AND HIS GUYS ARE COMIN' TOO?

OH YEAH, WE'RE CLOSE.

YOU SURE IT'S HIM? OKAY.

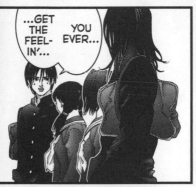

...GET THE FEEL-IN'...

YOU EVER...

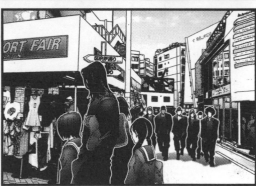

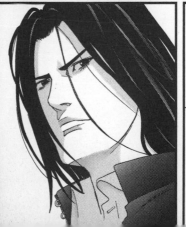

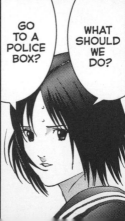

GO TO A POLICE BOX?

WHAT SHOULD WE DO?

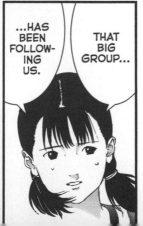

...HAS BEEN FOLLOW-ING US.

THAT BIG GROUP...

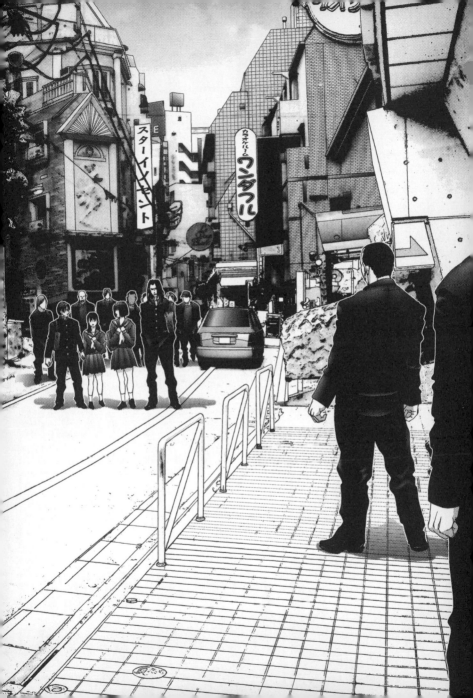

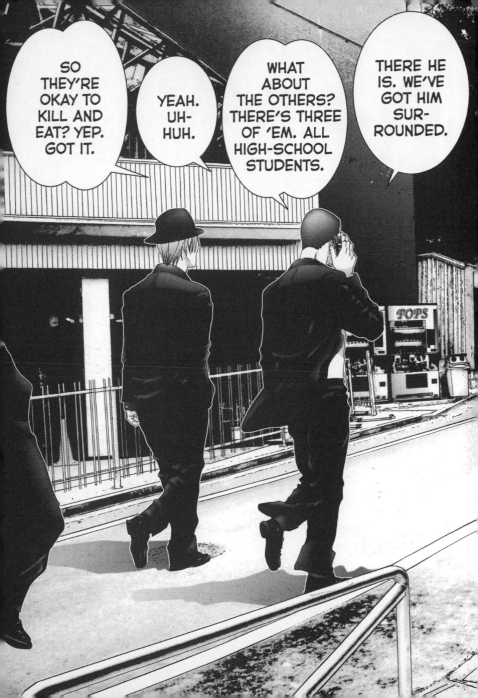

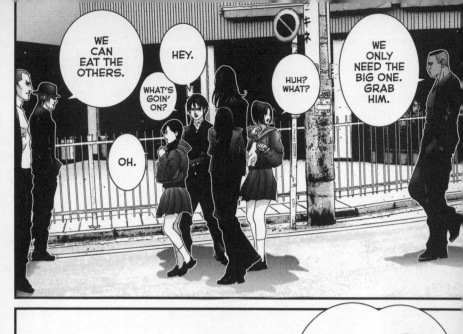

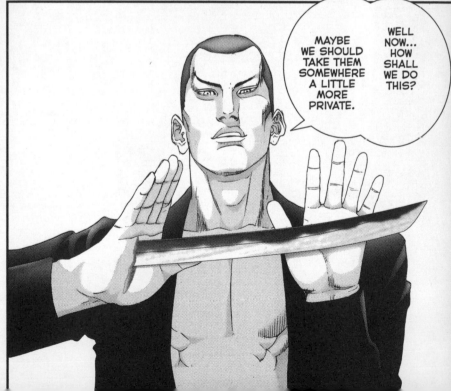

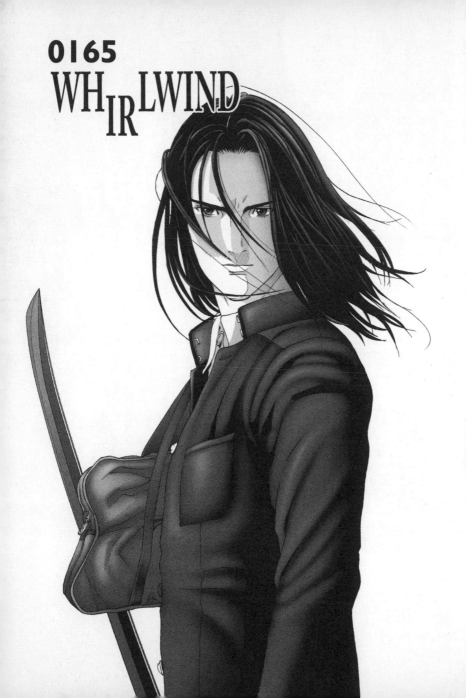

0165
WHIRLWIND

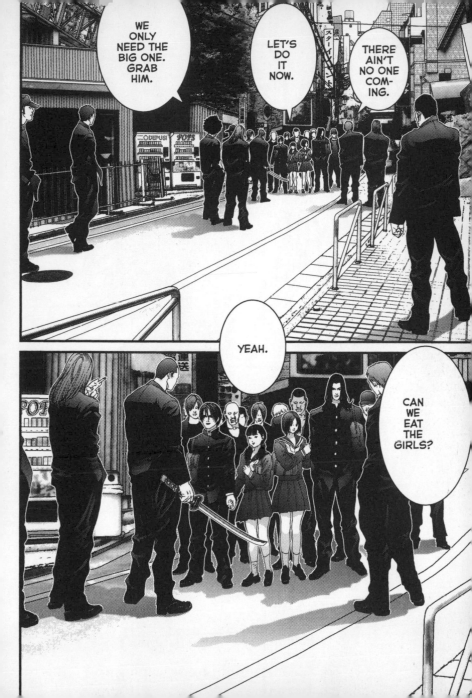

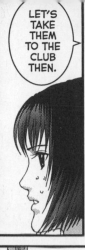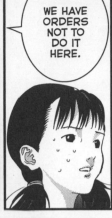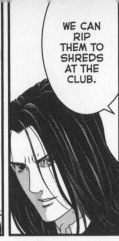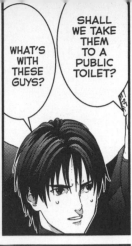

LET'S TAKE THEM TO THE CLUB THEN.

WE HAVE ORDERS NOT TO DO IT HERE.

WE CAN RIP THEM TO SHREDS AT THE CLUB.

WHAT'S WITH THESE GUYS?

SHALL WE TAKE THEM TO A PUBLIC TOILET?

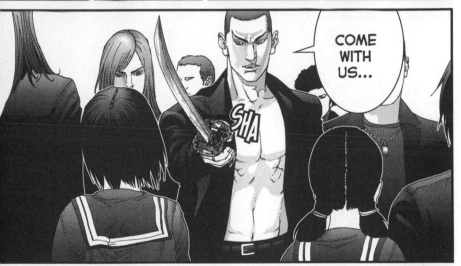

SHA

COME WITH US...

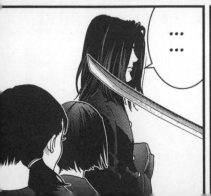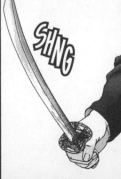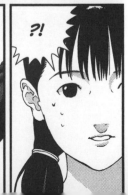

...
...

SHNG

?!

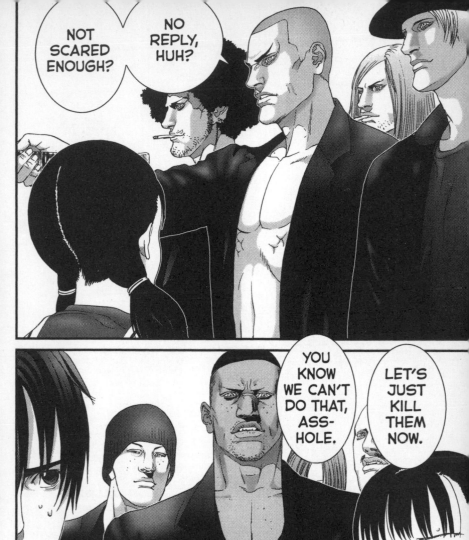
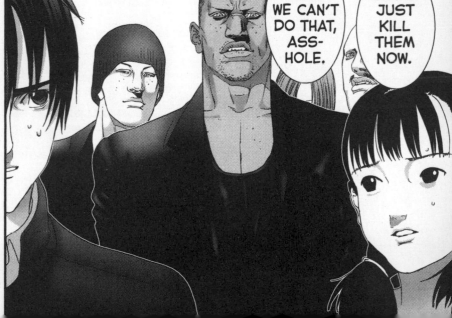

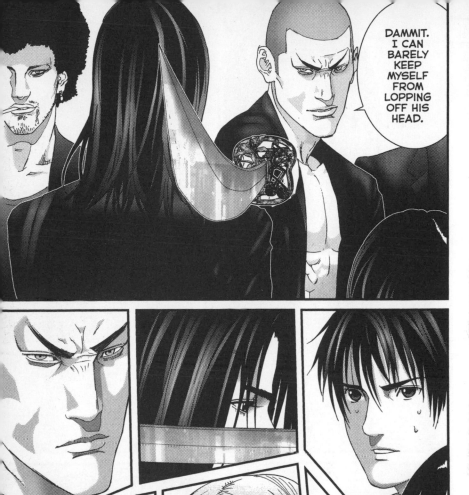

DAMMIT. I CAN BARELY KEEP MYSELF FROM LOPPING OFF HIS HEAD.

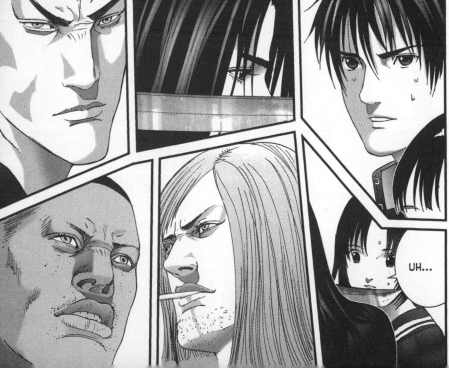

UH...

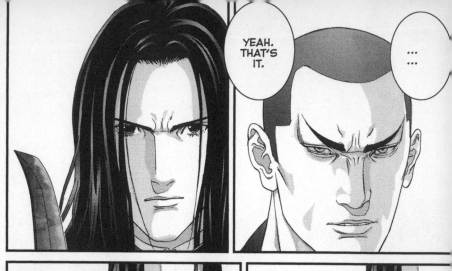

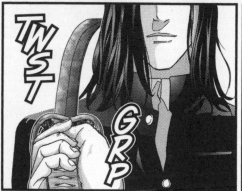

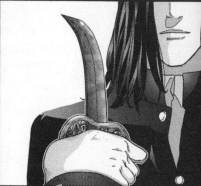

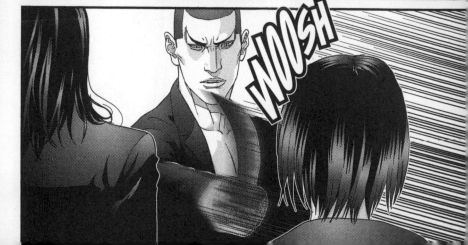

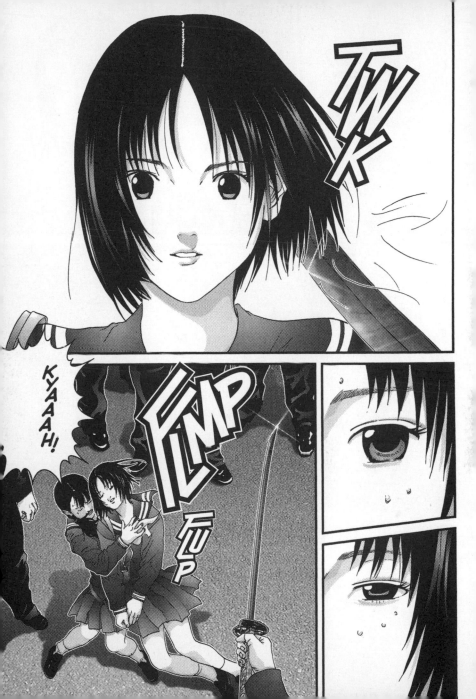

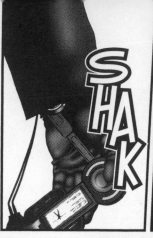
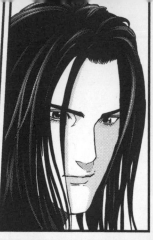
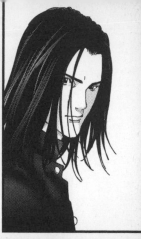

SHAK

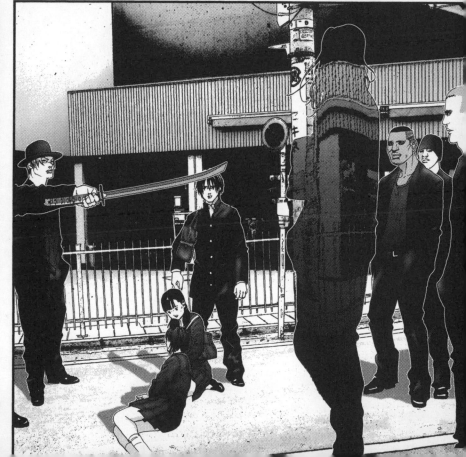

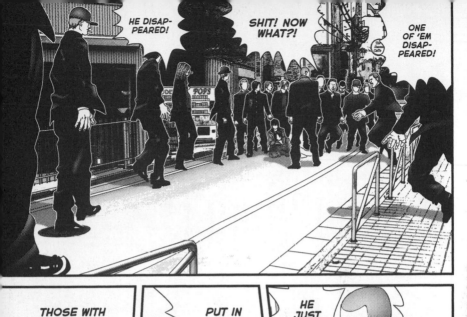

HE DISAP-
PEARED!

SHIT! NOW
WHAT?!

ONE
OF 'EM
DISAP-
PEARED!

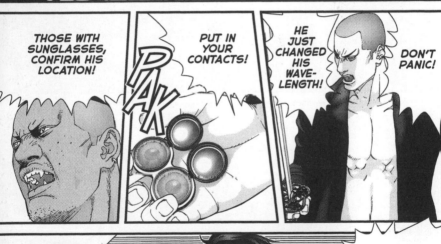

THOSE WITH
SUNGLASSES,
CONFIRM HIS
LOCATION!

PUT IN
YOUR
CONTACTS!

PAK

HE
JUST
CHANGED
HIS
WAVE-
LENGTH!

DON'T
PANIC!

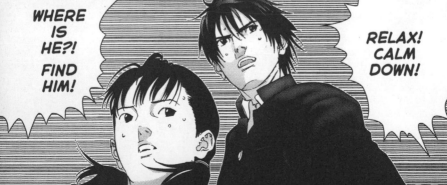

WHERE
IS
HE?!

FIND
HIM!

RELAX!
CALM
DOWN!

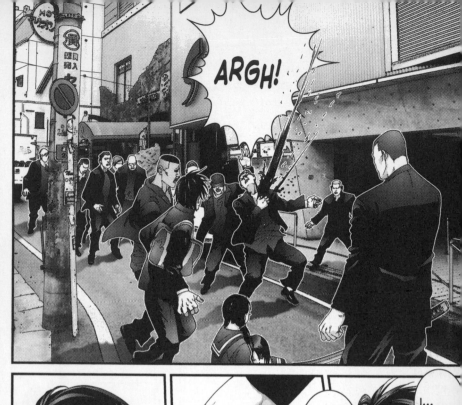

ARGH!

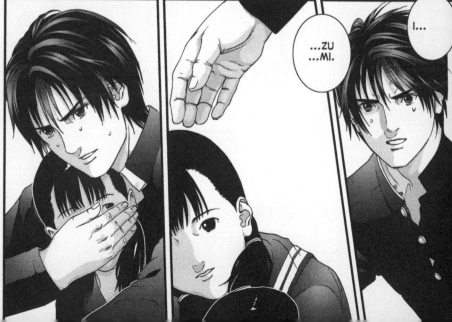

...ZU
...MI.

I...

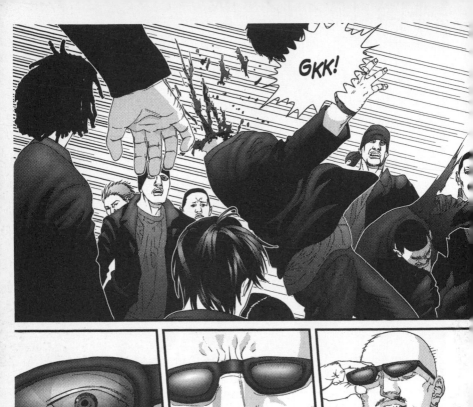

GKK!

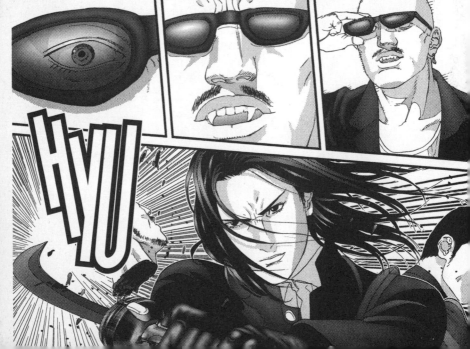

HYU

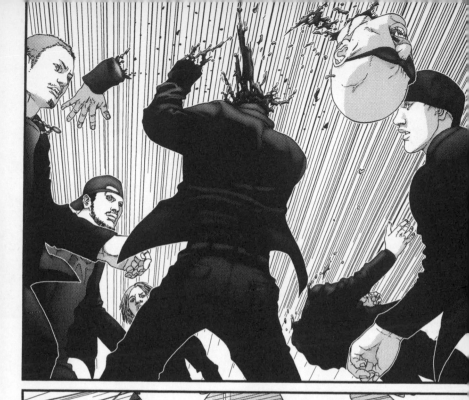

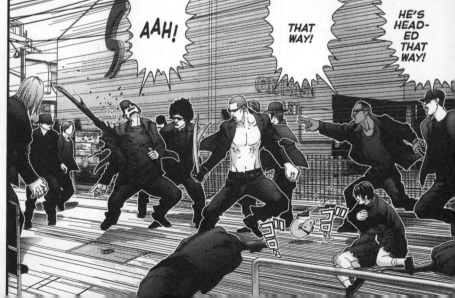

AAH!

THAT WAY!

HE'S HEADED THAT WAY!

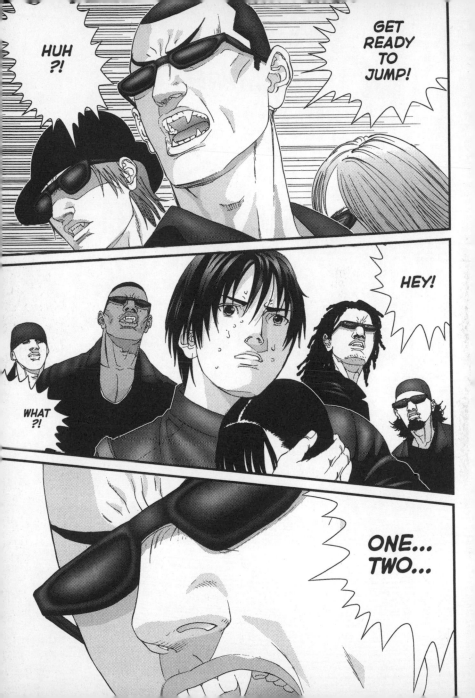

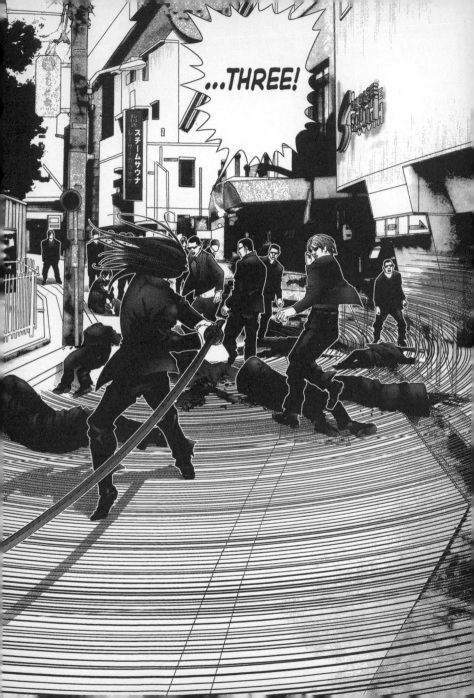

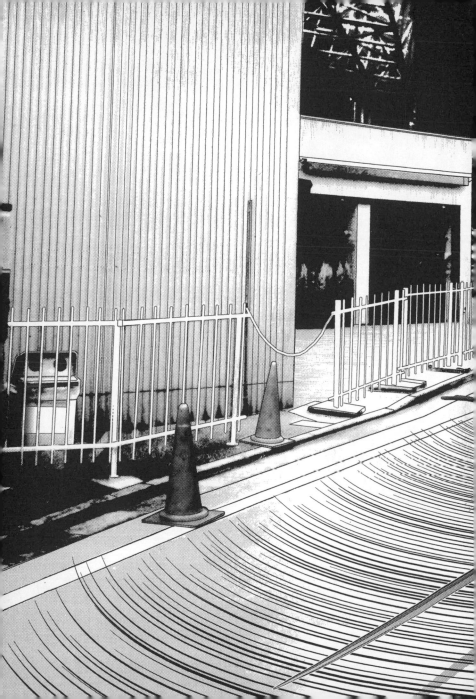

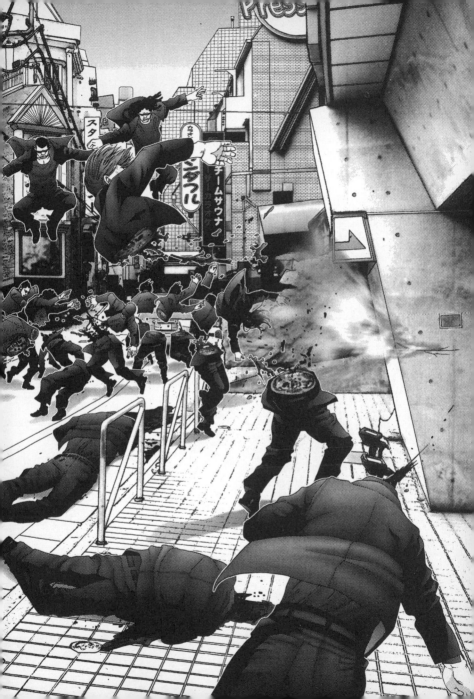

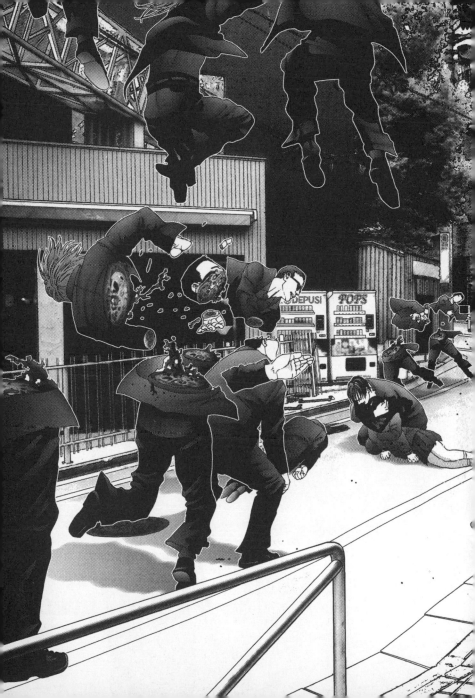

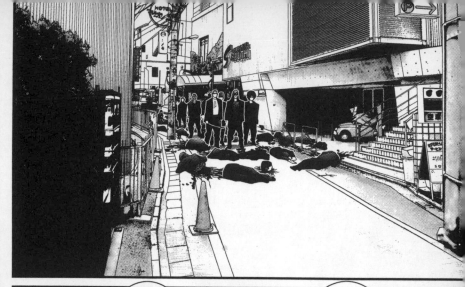

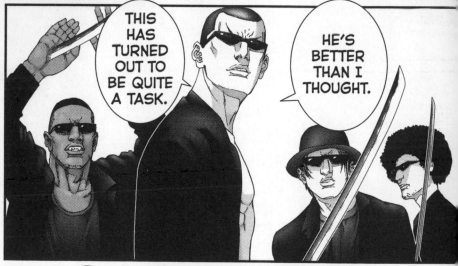

THIS HAS TURNED OUT TO BE QUITE A TASK.

HE'S BETTER THAN I THOUGHT.

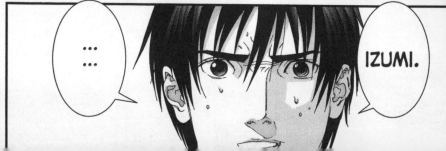

...
...

IZUMI.

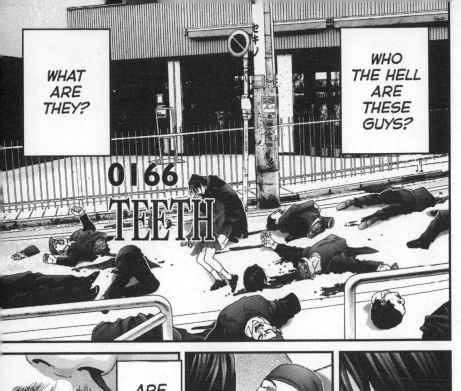

WHAT ARE THEY?

WHO THE HELL ARE THESE GUYS?

0166
TEETH

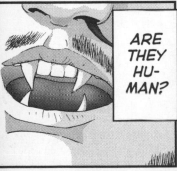

ARE THEY HUMAN?

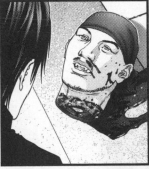

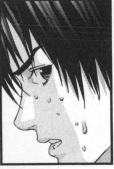

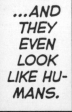

...AND THEY EVEN LOOK LIKE HUMANS.

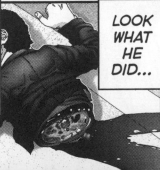

LOOK WHAT HE DID...

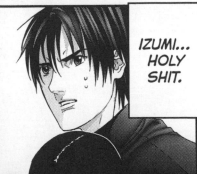

IZUMI... HOLY SHIT.

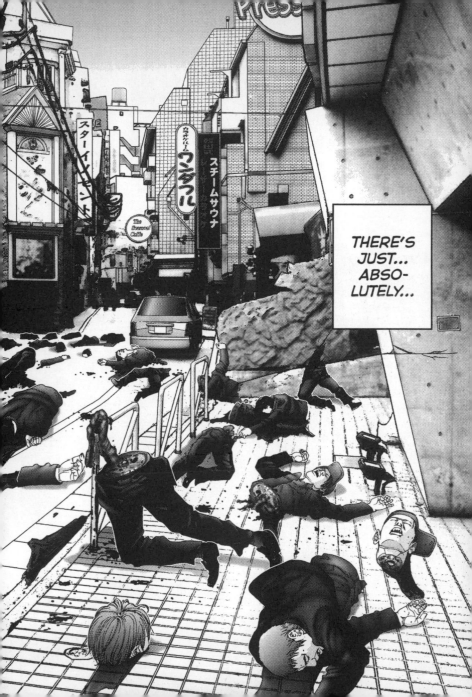

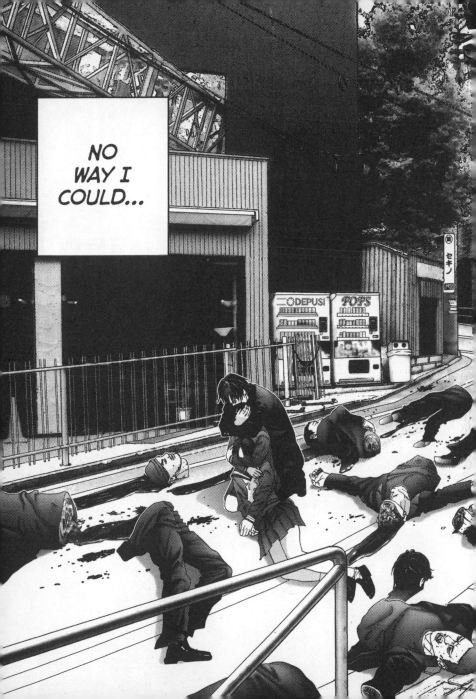

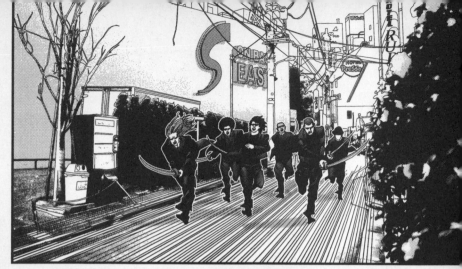

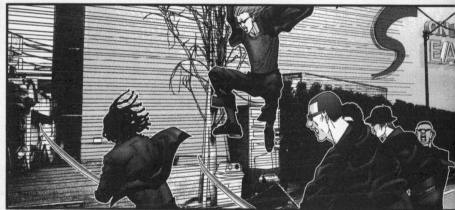

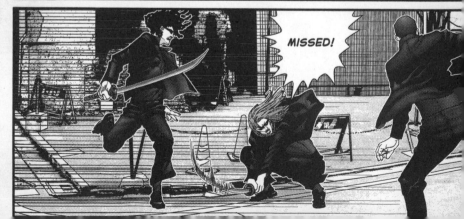

MISSED!

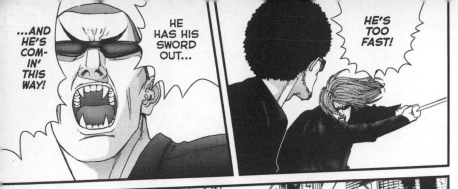

...AND HE'S COMIN' THIS WAY!

HE HAS HIS SWORD OUT...

HE'S TOO FAST!

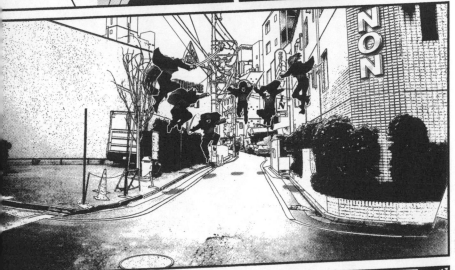

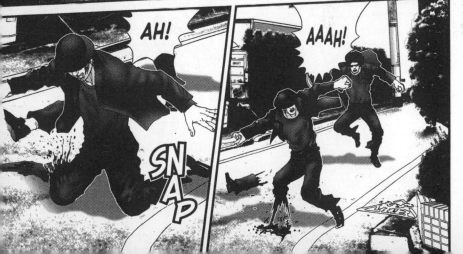

AH!

SNAP

AAAH!

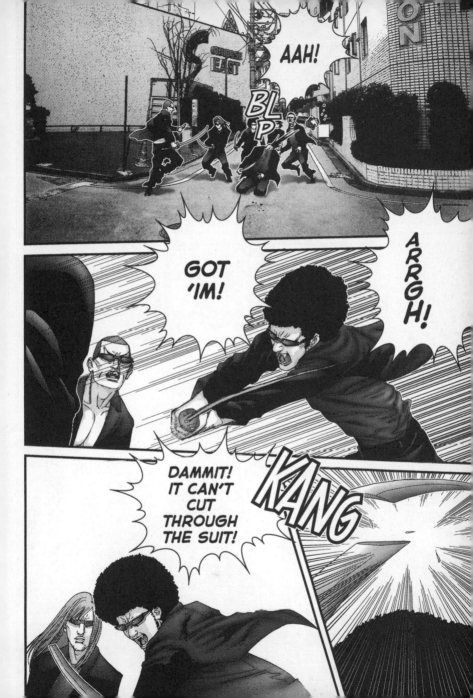

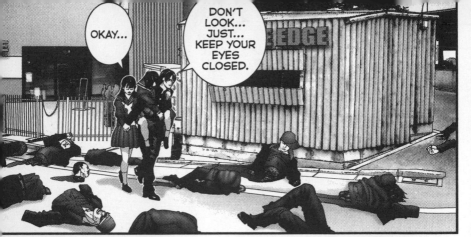

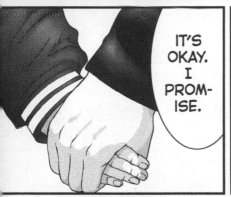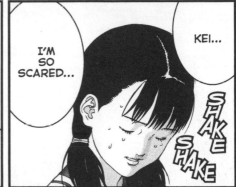

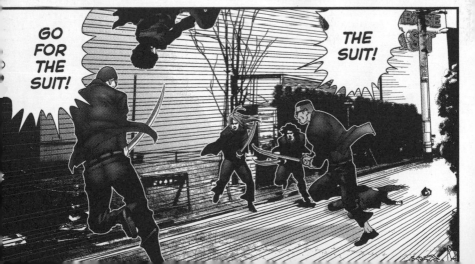

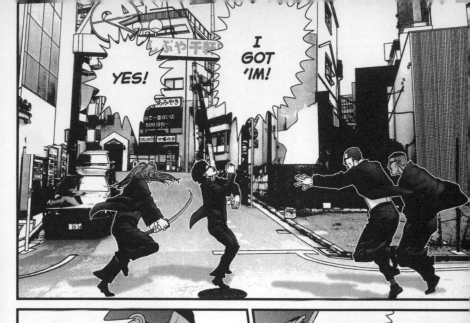

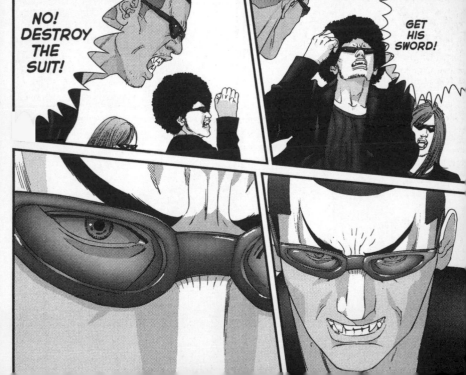

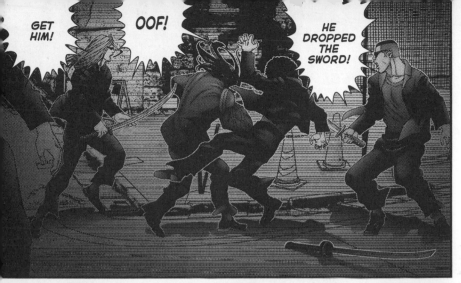

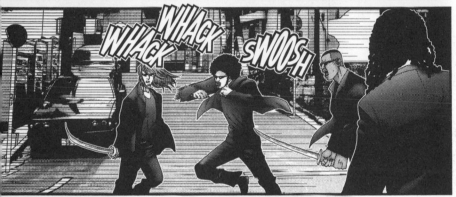

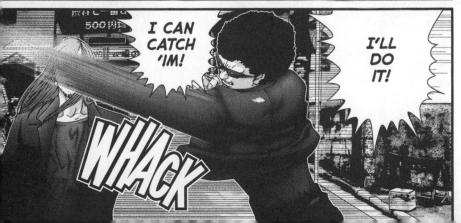

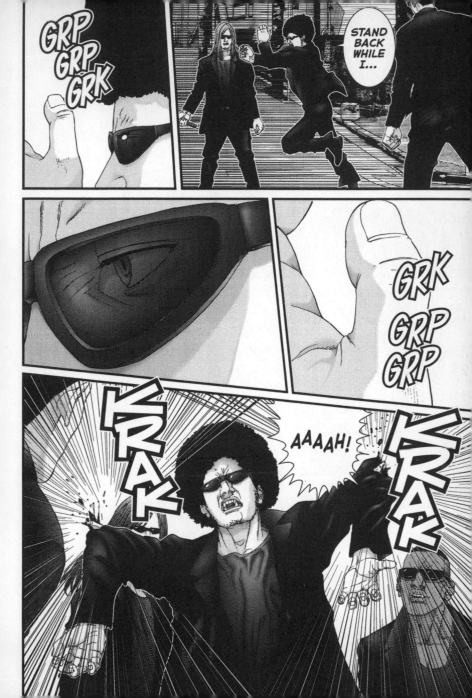

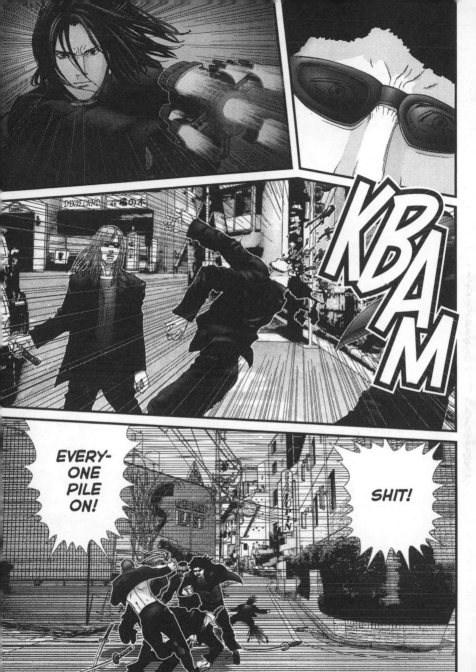

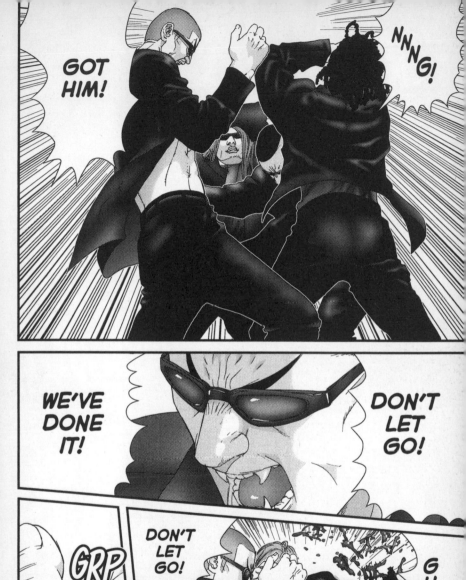
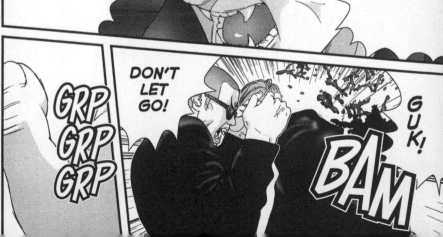

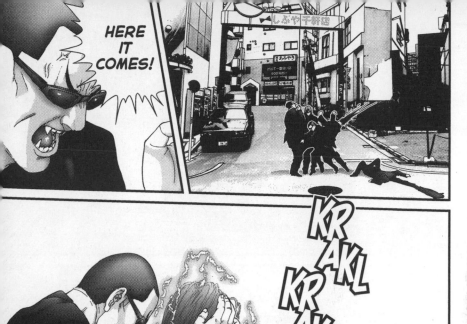

HERE
IT
COMES!

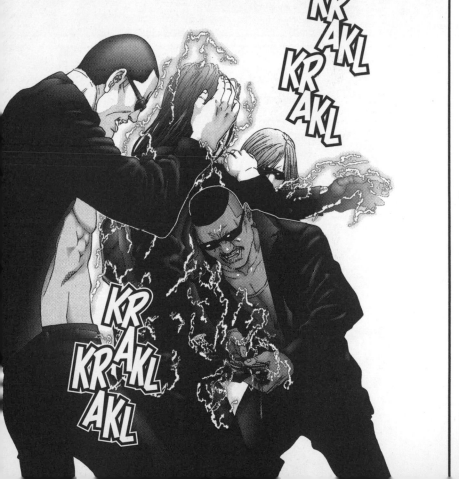

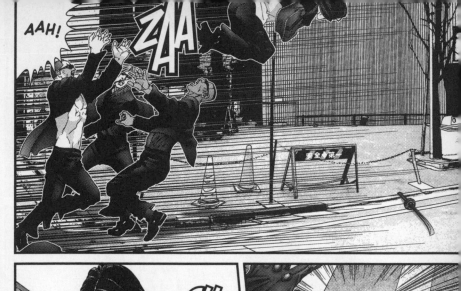

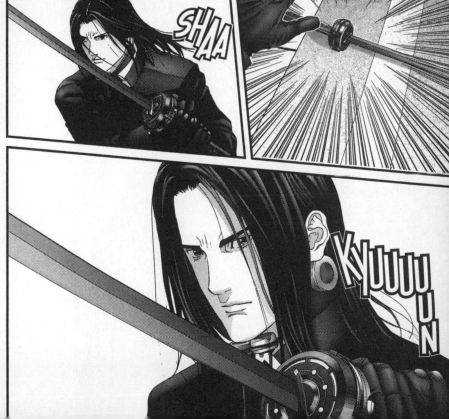

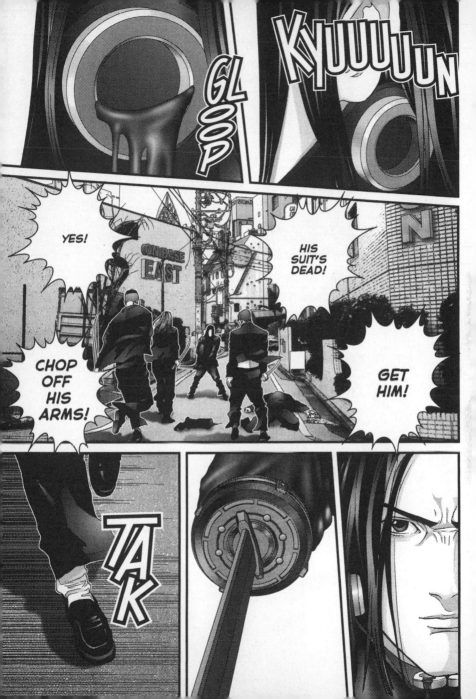

NNNNN!

ARGH!

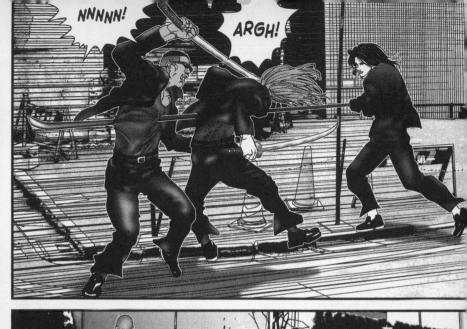

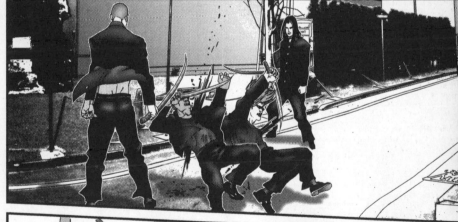

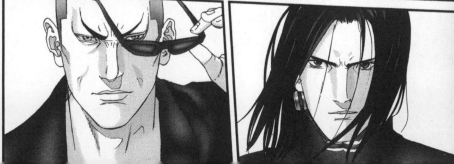

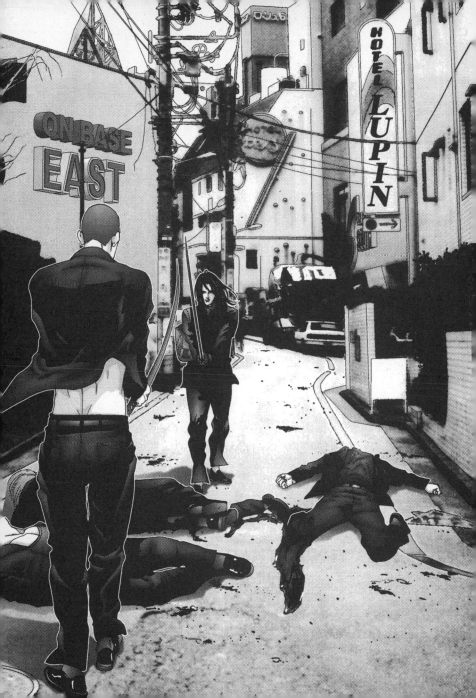

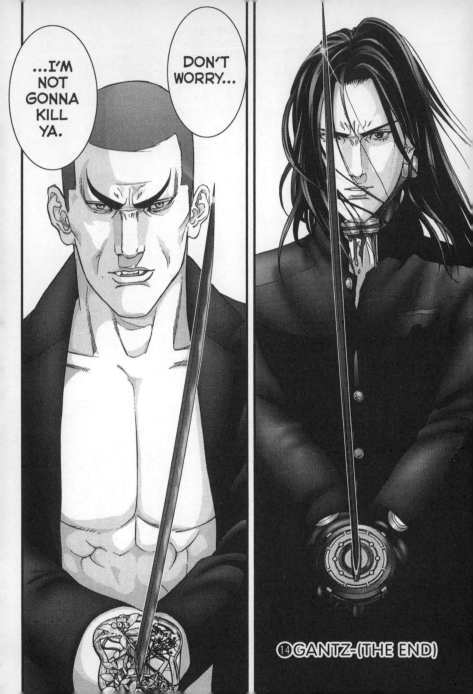

THANK YOU FOR TAKING
THE TIME TO DRAW YOUR
OWN ALIENS AND SEND THEM IN.

HERE'S THE BEST TEN.

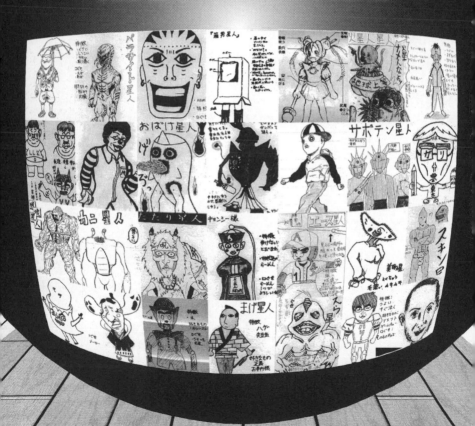

#10

ROVER ALIEN

Atom Kobo,
Saitama Prefecture

Excellent drawing skills.

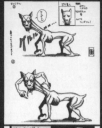

Characteristics
Catches things fast
Likes bones

Catch phrase:
"Grrr—eat!"

#9

LONGHORN BEETLE ALIEN

Hiroshi Kawasaki,
Hyogo Prefecture, 18

The drawing is too good
for words. It's too detailed.

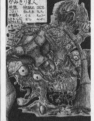

Characteristics
Strong, thinks of others
Likes eyeballs, stink bugs

Catch phrase:
"Kakkammokkomunma!"

#8

CHAMELEON ALIEN

Tomohiro Okano,
Saitama Prefecture

Too much effort
put into drawing.

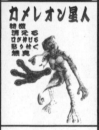

Characteristics
Disappears
Eyes extend
Gloms onto things
Odorless

#7

OKAMEN ALIEN

Manneken Pis,
Fukuoka Prefecture

At least it's original.

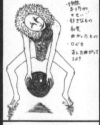

Characteristics
Funny way of running
Likes Japanese food,
curved things

Catch phrase:
"You're twisted?"

#6

ROLE-PLAY ALIEN

Ryuji Ando, Gifu Prefecture

Look at that perspective!

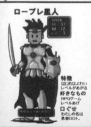

Characteristics
Starts out weak
Increases with levels
Likes RPG games, new levels

Catch phrase:
"My name is Yusha Roroto!"

#5

SEVEN SWORD ALIEN
Shinji Nakamoto, Tokyo, 25

Drawing is too poor for your age. Too many spelling mistakes.

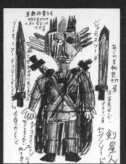

Characteristics
Justice sword
Bloody sword
Made of space metals (listed twice)
Can split the town in half
Manipulates wind and lightning

#4

BOX BOY ALIEN
Akira Toshida, Tokyo

Just like Tamao.

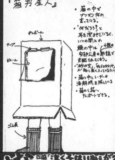

Characteristics
Mopes in a box
Seems to be saying something
Goes from box to box
Can teleport

#3

NAMAHAGE ALIEN
Mr. 92, Akita Prefecture

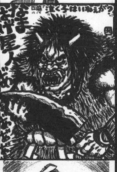

Characteristics
Looks like a woodblock print
Catch phrase is too much like real thing

Catch phrase:
"Are there any crying children here?"

#2

EBISU ALIEN
Kenta Miyajima, Tokyo, 17

Don't mess with the seven gods of fortune.

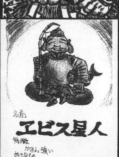

Characteristics
Puts up with a lot
Likes sake

Catch phrase:
"Ha ha ha ha ha"

And now, for number one . . . drumroll, please . . .

#1

NOVA ALIEN • DAVID ALIEN

Taro Nakagawa, Saitama Prefecture, 19

As you know, these are very famous statues. They could be used as—is, and I might just do so in the future.

Still, I'll have to think of what to do with the crotch. He could just look like some guy in a manga with no pants on.

That could be a problem . . .

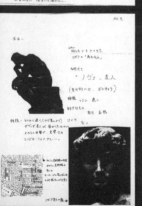

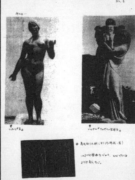

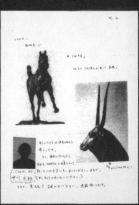

translation MATTHEW JOHNSON
lettering and retouch STUDIO CUTIE

publisher MIKE RICHARDSON

editor TIM ERVIN

book design STEPHEN REICHERT

Published by Dark Horse Comics, Inc., in association with Shueisha, Inc.

Dark Horse Manga
A division of Dark Horse Comics, Inc.
10956 SE Main Street
Milwaukie, OR 97222

darkhorse.com
First edition: November 2010
ISBN 978-1-59582-598-8

1 3 5 7 9 10 8 6 4 2

Printed at Transcontinental Gagné, Louiseville, QC, Canada

GANTZ
[ガンツ]
⑭

Original cover design: Yoshiyuki Seki for VOLARE, Inc.

To find a comics shop in your area, call the Comic Shop Locator Service toll-free at 1-888-266-4226.

MIKE RICHARDSON President and Publisher • NEIL HANKERSON Executive Vice President • TOM WEDDLE Chief Financial Officer • RANDY STRADLEY Vice President of Publishing • MICHAEL MARTENS Vice President of Business Development • ANITA NELSON Vice President of Business Affairs • MICHA HERSHMAN Vice President of Marketing • DAVID SCROGGY Vice President of Product Development • DALE LAFOUNTAIN Vice President of Information Technology • DARLENE VOGEL Director of Purchasing • KEN LIZZI General Counsel • DAVEY ESTRADA Editorial Director • SCOTT ALLIE Senior Managing Editor • CHRIS WARNER Senior Books Editor • DIANA SCHUTZ Executive Editor • CARY GRAZZINI Director of Design and Production • LIA RIBACCHI Art Director • CARA NIECE Director of Scheduling

STOP!

止 ま れ

THIS IS THE BACK OF THE BOOK!

This manga collection is translated into English but oriented in right-to-left reading format at the creator's request, maintaining the artwork's visual orientation as originally published in Japan. If you've never read manga in this way before, take a look at the diagram below to give yourself an idea of how to go about it. Basically, you'll be starting in the upper right corner and will read each balloon and panel moving right to left. It may take some getting used to, but you should get the hang of it very quickly. Have fun!

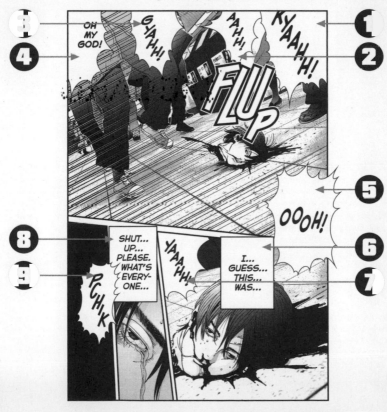